Moments
of Knowing

Moments
of Knowing

A Memoir

Mary Helen Fein

SHE WRITES PRESS

Published 2025

Printed in the United States of America

Print ISBN: 978-1-64742-862-4
E-ISBN: 978-1-64742-863-1
Library of Congress Control Number: 2024923448

For information, address:
She Writes Press
1569 Solano Ave #546
Berkeley, CA 94707

Interior design and typeset by Katherine Lloyd, The DESK

She Writes Press is a division of SparkPoint Studio, LLC.

I dedicate this book to my husband,
Stuart Allen Clancy.
He has been my constant support
and my most kindred spirit.

First Moment
of Knowing

I had my first moment of knowing when I was five years old. The year was 1948. I was in first grade at Joseph R. Lamar Elementary School in Augusta, Georgia. It was a warm, sunny day, and we were outside for recess. I was standing around, not doing anything in particular.

Across the playground, I saw Marilyn Cloud, the most popular girl in the class. I thought her name was beautiful, and I imagined that, like her name, she was perfect, too. She was everything I was not. I had a stupid name no one had ever heard of: Mary Helen. I was too big; I was too shy. I wore hand-me-downs from neighbors, and my mother permed my hair into tight ugly curls, which I hated. Marilyn Cloud, in contrast, was tiny, confident, and blond. She had cascading golden curls, and she wore a perfect outfit every day.

As I was thinking these thoughts, I must have stared at her too long because suddenly I was horrified to see she had noticed me. Her head snapped in my direction, and her face transformed into the expression of a hawk with prey in its sights: squinting eyes, one eyebrow slightly raised, pursed lips. Leaning toward one of the many girls allowed to follow her around, she said something that made them all laugh. They looked at me, whispering behind their hands and giggling.

I moved quickly from horror to panic when I realized Marilyn Cloud was marching in my direction, her entourage close behind.

"Hi, Hairy Melon." I cringed at this rendition of my name, which was followed by whoops of laughter. No one had ever called me that before. I had never even thought of it. I tried not to see myself as half a red watermelon, with curly black hair growing all over it.

Marilyn was just getting started. "Where did you find your clothes? In someone's garbage?"

Just to put my eyes somewhere else, I looked down at my feet, hoping no one would realize how ashamed I felt. Gazing downward, I became conscious of my shoes, of the ground, of my not-so-white-anymore socks. My brown oxfords had black tape holding them together where the shoe had come away from the sole. I felt removed from everyone around me as I contemplated my footwear.

Marilyn Cloud followed my gaze, then pointed at my shoes for everyone to see. She kept her arm pointing at me as she twisted around to face her crowd. "Aw, poor Hairy Melon, I'll just have to tell my momma to take up a collection in church to get her some new shoes." More peals of laughter.

Then, in an instant, she lost interest. Her head swiveled about as she scanned the playground for her next victim. My heart pounded as she marched away, sweeping her retinue behind.

I walked over to a brick wall and found a corner where no one could see that I was crying. I shook inside, but I gradually calmed down. I forced myself to stop the tears and scrubbed at my eyes with both fists.

First Moment of Knowing

How can someone be so mean? I asked myself. And then the next thought, *I will never, ever be mean like that. Never, ever, not to anyone.* This simple vow rose up of its own accord with a surprising strength.

I repeated the words to myself. "*I will never, ever . . .*" It was the repetition that set off the moment of knowing. I was making a vow. My five-year-old heart was fully engaged. *I am going to be the opposite of mean. I am going to be loving. I am going to be good to people. I am going to live for love.*

All the shame was left behind as I stepped into a higher world.

That vow never changed.

Behind
the Couch

Patricia told me to get behind the couch and crouch down so they wouldn't see me. Patricia was Preacher Williams's twelve-year-old daughter from next door who babysat me sometimes after she got home from school. Patricia was much taller than me and pretty. She was always nice to me. She had long, dark hair and kind, blue eyes. I always hoped to grow up to be just like her.

That night, we were both afraid. Patricia ran over to make sure the front screen door was latched. Sixteen-year-old Annie was out there in the dark with six or eight of her friends who came to help her. We could just see the shapes of them, hanging off an old jalopy. The weather was so hot, we couldn't even close the door. They came up to the porch.

Mommy said don't let Annie or her friends into the house, but there were only two of us and so many of them. Why did Mommy have to leave me alone with just Patricia? I was hiding behind the couch. I could see the weave of the beige upholstery fabric inches from my face. The floor was shiny, cream-colored linoleum, cold under my hands and feet. The big couch was soft and solid. It felt safe to be behind it.

This was Augusta, Georgia, and it was 1948. I was five years old. We were white, and Annie was Black. All of her friends on the porch were Black. Someone being Black made a big difference to Mommy and Art. It was okay for a Black person to work for them. It was okay for a Black person to be kind of an underling. But Black people could never be friends or neighbors. No Black people lived on our street, or went to our church, or went to my school.

That day had been Annie's first day on her new job, taking care of me while Mommy and Art went to work. Annie had been so nice and friendly. She was sixteen years old. She told me she had quit school so she could work and make money and start her real life. She was pretty and she smelled like perfume.

The whole time she was with me, she was nice to me. She smiled and gave me chocolate chip cookies for lunch. But then she left before I even finished eating. It didn't seem right to me, and I was a little scared being all by myself the whole afternoon.

But that night Annie was on the porch with five or six of her friends. They screamed and yelled, saying bad words and banging on the house with their fists. I had no idea what they were trying to tell us. I just hoped they didn't get into the house and find me and kill both of us.

Why would Mommy hire someone as young as Annie to stay with me every day? The daytime was when Mommy and Art went off to Fort Gordon, where Art did his army job stuff. He was more important now, since he had his big promotion ceremony.

We had to watch the whole thing. It was boring and too hot, but Mommy and I stayed until the end, standing in the sun for hours. There were flags, and red, white, and blue banners hanging around the outdoor stage. Art was blond and tall.

Mommy asked me in a whispered voice when I first met him, "Don't you think he's handsome?"

Moments of Knowing

At age five, I hadn't thought much about men being handsome, so I just nodded and smiled. Art stood up very straight when the officers gave him his certificate of promotion.

But it turned out that Art hated me. Mommy loved me, but she needed Art. So, she had to be on his side more than on mine.

Maybe it was his idea to get Annie to watch me every day.

My mommy was very beautiful. Everyone knew that, and everyone always told her and told me how beautiful she was. She had green eyes and long, dark hair and such a pretty face. She was not too tall or too short, not too fat or too thin. She had a magical smile that I loved to see. And I loved it when she put her arms around me and gave me a hug.

Mommy said Annie stole all her jewelry and that's why Annie left early before Mommy and Art got home from work. Both of them were surprised and angry that I was home all alone. They went around the house checking everything, pulling out dresser drawers, opening up cupboards and trying to discover everything what was missing—the pin from Granny, all of Art's army medals, the silvery metal cream pitcher and sugar bowl, and a lot of other stuff.

Mommy always made a funny joke reversing the names and calling them the "pream critcher" and the "booger shoal." But on that day, nothing was funny. Art yelled at me a little bit.

"You probably drove her away being a bad girl like you always are." He was trying to say it was my fault Annie left, but I just lay down on the floor and covered my head with my arms. After a while he left me alone.

They called the police. Two policemen came in dark blue uniforms with gold buttons. I found a place nearby to watch and listen. Everyone talked grown-up talk, so I didn't understand much. Then they got Patricia from next door to come over and stay with me, again. The grownups got into their car, and the police left. Then it was just me and Patricia.

Art and Mommy told Patricia they were going down to the other side of town to find "that little bitch," they called her, and make her give the stuff back.

"Now if they come here while we're gone, y'all don't let them in. Don't you dare open that screen door," Mommy said. "She might throw all the jewelry and the other things she stole on the floor, and then she could say she never took any of it, you hear me now? Whatever you do, don't let her in. Don't open that screen door."

Mommy and Art left, and it wasn't ten minutes before the old jalopy pulled up outside.

Annie came up to the house and stood outside the screen door. I stayed behind the couch because I was trembling and needed to stay in one place. They couldn't see me, so they didn't know I was there. They wouldn't think of killing me; instead, they would probably only think of killing Patricia because she was in front of the screen door, and they could see her. I hoped they didn't kill her because she was real nice. She's even the one who told me that time about how the man puts his thing in the woman and that's what makes babies.

Annie rattled the locked screen door and yelled, "Unlock this goddamn screen door, girl, or you gonna be sorry!" I could hear the flimsy door, and it felt like the whole house was rattling. Everyone was hollering, and Annie was still banging on the woodwork and pulling on the screen door handle. I was scared that the screen door was going to rip right off, just like it did that time when Art got so angry and jerked it too hard.

I peeked out around the side of the couch. Patricia looked as scared as me. She backed away from the front door and all the people. Her eyes were huge, and she looked ready to run out the back door and go home. They still didn't know I was behind the couch. They couldn't see me. My heart pounded so loud, I was afraid they would hear it. I didn't know what they wanted—maybe just to throw the jewelry on the floor, like Mommy said—but probably to kill us.

One of her friends handed Annie a bag. She turned it upside down and dumped everything out onto the porch floor.

Mommy was right. Annie wanted to get rid of everything that she had taken, so that no one could prove she stole it.

I saw some shiny jewelry, and I hoped the pream critcher wasn't dented.

Once they dumped the stuff on the porch, they piled back into the jalopy and left. The car disappeared up the street into the dark night, with everyone still yelling. We could hear them, but it was getting quieter. The sound stopped once they turned the corner at the end of the street.

Patricia came behind the couch and hugged me. I hugged her back, so happy they had left, but I was too scared to come out yet. She brought me a blanket, and I lay down right there on the floor behind the couch. She stroked my head.

I looked up at her and said proudly, "We never opened that screen door."

The Fifties

Three years later, when I was eight years old, Art drove us across the country from Georgia to California. We were moving because Art was a career army officer, and he was being sent to help fight the war in Korea. Perhaps my mother wanted to live someplace other than Georgia where she had grown up. But because I didn't have a clear idea of the size of the Pacific Ocean, I thought she wanted to live on the West Coast so she would be near Art while he was in Korea.

I remember the drive across Texas because it seemed to take weeks. The landscape was endlessly the same, with the highway going up and down hills that were at least a hundred feet high. It was an undulating gray strip of road. Nothing on either side of the road, just scrubby brown flats and mountains in the distance.

We stopped at Carlsbad Caverns in New Mexico. I saw stalactites and stalagmites, and even remembered which was which, possibly for an entire day. We crossed the border into Ciudad Juarez, Mexico, and I discovered that our country wasn't the only country in the world. The streets of Juarez weren't paved, and the town was busy and crowded. The sound of people speaking Spanish in the background was like a new kind of music.

The first place we lived in California was Redondo Beach, a small town about twenty miles south of Los Angeles. My uncle and his family lived there, and my mother wanted to be near her brother. I could walk a few blocks to the ocean, and I loved letting the giant waves roll over me and pound me into the sand and gravel. I didn't care if I came out bruised and beat up. I had spent time at Jones Beach when I was younger and still living in New York before my parents got divorced, but I had never experienced an ocean with power like this. The waves looked about ten feet high. They crashed over me and spun me around underwater. I couldn't get enough of it.

Sometimes, we would go to a concrete river. It was a strange sight—a concrete riverbed about ten feet wide with only a foot of water, flowing through town. I think it was the Los Angeles River. It was ugly, but I was a kid and didn't care. I brought a jar and caught tadpoles. I loved catching them with their wavy tails.

The best thing about our house in Redondo Beach was a small playhouse in the backyard. It was hardly big enough for a child-sized table and two little chairs. I remember playing in the little house with a girl my own age who lived nearby.

"What shall I make for dinner?" The playhouse kitchen had a tea set, so we could dine in style.

"You set the table and I'll cook." My friend would carefully put two plates on the table, and we both took our places at the table.

The best thing to have with a tea set was "real food." For a make-believe meal, invisible pretend food was insufficient. I had an idea, since an orange tree grew over the little playhouse.

"I think we should have steak and perhaps oranges? Yes, oranges would be very good with steak. You pick the oranges, and I'll go get the steak with those delicious steak bones." My friend would pick an orange for each of us and place them on our plates.

The Fifties

I would cross the backyard to a big bag tucked in a corner near the fence. We had just discovered the amazing second food source that we called "steak with bones." It was actually a large bag of dog biscuits shaped like cartoon bones. I reached into the bag, took out two steaks, then carried them back into our dining room and elegantly placed one on each plate.

"Dinner's ready! Come and get it," I called out in a singsong. My friend and I pulled our tiny chairs up to the table to enjoy our exciting real food. The dog biscuits weren't as tasty as the oranges, but we ate them anyway. We were thrilled that our playhouse meal had two kinds of food.

We parroted all the adult dinner table conversations we could think of. "How was your day? "Did you pick up the mail?" "Would you care for seconds?"

"The steak is a little overdone, don't you think?" I said.

"Oh no, it's just perfect," replied my friend.

The dog bones were dry with a grainy, cardboard taste. But that didn't matter. What mattered was having dinner in our beautiful home with a real plate and real food. Too good to be true.

A few years later it was 1954, and I was eleven years old, old enough to have been assigned the chore of ironing clothes. It was morning, and Mommy was at work. I set up the ironing board in the kitchen, where I could look out the windows and see what was happening in the neighborhood. The radio was playing "Rock Around the Clock." It was the first time I had heard that song. Right away, I knew I was hearing a kind of music that hadn't existed before, music that belonged to me, to people my own age. It was my first realization that I was part of a new generation. This music was ours . . . our setting, our landscape. From that moment, I was conscious of being part of a group in time. There were no words to describe us yet, no "hippies," no "baby boomers." But my awareness of belonging started with that song.

It was only rock and roll. Not Frank Sinatra anymore. Not our parents' music. Something timely, something happening fast. Bill Haley and the Comets counting the rock and roll hours: one, two, three, four . . . I immediately knew I was connected to those words and that sound. Across that connection, information flowed to me for the rest of my life. I was proud of my generation at that moment, and I stayed proud of us. We were about freedom.

At about that time, we moved away from Redondo Beach because rent was lower elsewhere. My mother went back to college. She wanted a degree that would lead to a better paying job. To pay for school, she needed cheaper housing. We moved to Long Beach to the Carmelitos Housing Project. This was a place for poor people—government-subsidized units, much cheaper than Redondo. Our family was just Mommy and us three kids. Art was still in Korea.

Mommy had had two more children, with Art. Savannah had been born in Georgia and was an infant-in-arms when Art drove us across the country. Savannah was only two years old, nine years younger than I was. Mommy's other younger child was Artie, which we all pronounced "RT." He was two years older than Savannah. They were both beautiful little toddlers. They had blue eyes and white-blond hair like their father. I helped take care of them, but while Mommy was at work all day, they went to a lady who lived nearby in the projects. The lady just sat them in front of the TV all day, but in 1954, that was childcare. Mommy worked as a bookkeeper in a jewelry store.

Living in the Carmelitos Projects was scary. It was a violent place. Everyone was poor and stressed. Mommy got angry at a neighbor boy for writing dirty words on the sidewalk near our front door. To teach him a lesson, she took his bike and locked it in our kitchen, where it could be seen through the window. The next day she was at work, but I was home alone when the boy and two of his friends came by. The three of them broke a window and came into the house. They took his bike and threatened me and Mommy. I was so scared that I crawled under the kitchen table trying to be invisible. They said they were going to beat me up and Mommy, too, sometime soon.

"Just you wait."

I cowered under the table, afraid the boys would hit me. I was shaking when they finally left with the bike.

I told Mommy what happened when she got home, but it seemed like she was too tired from her long day to do anything about it. We saw the boys around, as they lived nearby, and I was always scared they would turn on me and fulfill their threat. But they ignored us from then on.

I didn't realize that the daily violence in the Carmelitos Projects was changing my view of the world. The world had once been a safe place. But no more.

Summers
in New York

Each year in June, as soon as school was out, I would fly from California to New York to stay with my father for the summer. I always loved coming East and leaving behind the hard life with my mother. My dad lived with his mother—my Nana—in the house where he was born. This house was on Tyndall Avenue, a leafy, tree-lined street, green and peaceful, and somehow still within the New York city limits.

The house still stands today in Riverdale, the small, northernmost part of the Bronx along the Hudson River.

I loved being in Riverdale, in contrast to my mother's rough California setting. Everyone was friendly on the streets. No one was ever threatening or mean. I felt safe.

Most of all, I loved being in Nana's kitchen. She let me have a turkey sandwich for breakfast any time I wanted, my favorite. I would sit on the long bench at the kitchen table, with her on the other bench across from me. A green and white metal bread box with a roll top, like a desk, was on the counter behind me. A *pushkah*, or charity box, hung on the wall close to the table. All the grown-ups would drop in a coin or two whenever they were at the table, to support the Holy Land of Israel. These boxes were a way to teach charity in Jewish homes.

Summers in New York

There was a narrow butler's pantry, lined with glass-doored cabinets for china dishes. The butler's pantry served as a hallway into the dining room. Usually, only Nana and I were home, and I had the run of the house. I loved to play pickup sticks on the floor of the dining room. First, I would retrieve one of Nana's red, faceted drinking glasses from a wooden cabinet. This special drinking glass was full of multicolored swizzle sticks from various New York City clubs and bars. My dad was one of eight siblings, most of them twenty-somethings, working in the city and exploring New York's clubs and nightlife, bringing home these tokens of their experiences.

These swizzle sticks were my best-ever pickup sticks.

To play the game, someone holds all the pickup sticks in one hand, so they stand vertically. Then they quickly pull their hand away, and the sticks fall into a random pile, many of them atop others in crisscross jumbles. The game is to pick up one stick at a time without moving any others.

After many months of practice, I was good at it. An important move in this game is to pick up the top stick on a pile, without moving the ones beneath it. Usually, you do this by leveraging the top stick, pushing down on the end touching the floor, so that the other end lifts off the pile of sticks beneath it. Once your stick is no longer touching the pile beneath it, you can simply snatch it away without risk.

As much as I loved the kitchen and the dining room and my pickup sticks game, I loved cuddling on Nana's lap in the living room the best. She would read me stories from picture books. I felt at peace and contented.

I had friends along Tyndall Avenue. Mary Lou Merkle lived next door. She was my age and Catholic. The Tracys lived up the street. They were Catholic, too, and there were at least seven Tracy kids. I could recite their names in order: Billy, Bobby, Lynn,

Moments of Knowing

Kathy, Elizabeth, James, and Francis. We played together most days. Our primary activity was roller skating up and down the Tyndall Avenue sidewalk.

Sometimes we would gather on the six steps leading up to Tracy's house. We would play school. One person would be the teacher and stand at the foot of the steps and be in charge. We played Button, Button, Who's Got the Button. The teacher would put a button between her two hands, holding her hands as if in prayer. Each seated student extended their own praying hands. The teacher visited each student. When the teacher got to me, I would hold out my praying hands, and the teacher would slide both her hands in between my own. Sometimes she would drop the button into my hands. No one could see "who's got the button." It was exciting to be the one who had it.

After the teacher visited each student, the idea of the game was for the students to guess who had the button. We would all chant "Button, Button, Who's Got the Button?" When someone guessed right, they could move up to a higher step.

After playing games, we would eat penny candy. I remember candy paper—we called them dots. Dots came a on long sheet of white paper, about two inches wide. I'd pick the varied colored dots of candy off the paper and pop them into my mouth. There were also little individually wrapped Mary Janes in yellow paper and inch-high, red Coca Cola bottles made of wax, which contained a sweet liquid. There were Boston Baked Beans, which were bright red peanut candies, and there were candy cigarettes, very sophisticated. I didn't like the little Bonomo's Turkish Taffy bites much. Dots were my favorite.

A young woman who was about eighteen lived across the street. We heard she had become a nun. Her name was Kathleen Votay. I was astonished that regular people from my street could become nuns.

At the far end of the block was Dr. Berger's house. He was our doctor, and the grown-ups took me to see him the time we played, "Who Can Keep Bubble Gum Stuck Over Their Eye the Longest." I won this game, but then no one could get the big pink glob off my face, so we had to visit Dr. Berger to have it removed. I was happy that I had won, and I didn't mind having to get the gum removed by an MD.

Dr. Berger's son was named Adolf Berger. He was a few years older than I, so he was probably born around 1940. Today, I wonder why anyone would name their son Adolf at that time in history. Perhaps it was a family name being passed on to the next generation.

Berger is mostly a French name, pronounced with a soft g. It can be Jewish but isn't usually. In French, the name refers to shepherds who lived in the mountains or "bergs."

One other important person on our block was Howie Karger. Howie was my age. His father was also a doctor. The Kargers lived across from Nana's house. Howie was known as a bad boy. One day, he invited me in. I was a little scared because I knew he was a bad boy, but I was curious enough to ignore my fear and go into the house. No one seemed to be home, and we sat on the floor in his father's office.

He reached up to his father's bookshelves and took down a giant medical book with black and white photos. He opened it up to a picture of a naked man with close-ups of his genitals. I looked for a few moments, as I hadn't had such a clear view before. But I knew this was bad behavior, looking at pictures like this. I stood up and left Howie's house quickly. Of course, I never told anyone what happened. Until today.

Normally, every summer when I came East, I stayed at Nana's house. But in the summer of 1952, when I was nine years old, my father wanted to do something special. He rented a small but beautiful home about twenty minutes to the north, on a quiet street in White Plains, New York. He rented it for the summer and just for us. Nana's long-time housekeeper Hattie Mae came with us, and she took care of me every day while he was at work. She pronounced her name "Ahddie" Mae, so that's what we all called her. Ahddie Mae was Black. She was wide but not very tall. She was bent over with age and had gray hair that went in every direction. She had a kind face and a warm smile. I loved Ahddie Mae.

I was shooting up in height, so Ahddie Mae and I could just about look one another in the eye without her having to stoop down. I had known her all my life. I was always at ease when Ahddie Mae was with me. I felt safe.

The White Plains house had two stories. There was an arched front door with a little arched window. The hallway had a light wood floor and a mirror with an ornate gold frame. The mirror let someone take one last look to make sure they looked okay before going out into the world.

The kitchen was warm and friendly. There was a nook with a round table surrounded by banquette seating. I felt cozy and happy there. I watched Ahddie Mae make lunch, then enjoyed eating with her as she joined me. In the evenings, Ahddie Mae would serve Daddy and me in the dining room. We invited her to join us, but she said, "No, thank you." It wasn't her way. Not in 1952.

In the living room, there was a black, upright Steinway piano. What would become a life-long love of music was just beginning for me. I didn't know how to play piano yet, but I badly wanted lessons. I would peck at the keys.

One night after dinner, my father and I were sharing the piano bench. I was on the right where the high notes were. I showed him how I could slide the back of my hand across the keys all the way up to the top of the keyboard. My dad told me this was called a *glissando*. He had recently taught me to play the top part of the "Chopsticks" duet, and I loved it when we played that together.

"I want piano lessons so bad," I told him.

"When you're a little bit older, you can take lessons," he replied. My heart leapt. My wonderful father was saying "Yes" to my dream. My dream of playing piano. But even more, my dearest dream of coming to live with him and Nana all year round, even during the school year. I didn't have the courage to ask him if that would happen. What if he said no?

My father said, "Did you know that I took piano lessons when I was twelve? I wasn't very good, so it was just for a year. Then I joined the Ham Radio club and that was the end of piano. But I do remember just one piece of music."

"Play it for me! What is it?" I exclaimed, excited to learn he could actually play a real piece of music.

"It's called, 'Fur Elise,' which in German means, 'For Elise.' It's by Beethoven. They say Beethoven loved Elise, and that he wrote this just for her, but it was almost a hundred years ago, and he never got married to anyone, so no one knows for sure who Elise was."

"Oooh," I replied, moved by this mysterious story. I loved how romantic it was, and I liked that her identity was still a secret.

My dad played the piece beautifully. For the rest of the summer, there were many evenings when we enjoyed ourselves in the living room after dinner, and he would often play "Fur Elise." To this day, it's one of my most favorite compositions, one that I love to play.

In the daytime when my father was at work, I spent time in the backyard of the house. This yard was the most beautiful garden I had ever seen. A fragrant area of red roses led to a different area with pink and white peonies, one little garden after another. One of these gardens had a wooden bench, another an iron chair painted shiny dark green. Some of these outdoor nooks had elaborate greenery with delicate ferns, the perfect backdrop to colorful blossoms. All the little areas combined to display their colors like a bright abstract painting. Nana wasn't much of a gardener, and we had never even had a real yard in California, much less a garden. Being this close to zinnias, dahlias, petunias, and clematis was a new experience for me. I loved sitting in that garden, and I have loved flowers ever since then.

Most afternoons, I put on my bathing suit and walked half a block to the end of the street. A small pond welcomed everyone in the neighborhood. It wasn't deep, and it was completely placid. I went swimming most afternoons. A sandy beach about ten feet wide had plenty of room for everyone's beach towels to be spread out. I could lie in the sun until it got too hot. Then it was time to cool off. Wading into the water, my toes would encounter an unpleasant layer of squishy mud. But the water itself was so cool and pleasant that the mud was not a real deterrent. The pond was big enough to have a raft in the middle, and it was a small challenge for me to swim all the way out and pull myself up the ladder. I could lay down on the wooden boards of the raft to dry off and warm up in the sunshine. After an hour or two at the pond, I was back at the house, clean and ready for my dad to come home from work.

The house had a den with a black and white TV. This was unusual in 1952. I had never seen a TV before, and it was exciting to be allowed to watch *Howdy Doody* a few times. I loved Princess Summerfall Winterspring. I think it was her name I loved the most.

Summers in New York

John Kennedy was on TV for some reason, getting a reputation in politics. I remember watching him with Daddy and Ahddie Mae. They were both interested in him, so I was, too. None of us knew that seeing JFK was a glimpse into the future.

I was just beginning to read for pleasure. Ahddie Mae took me to the local library, and I got my first library card. The next weekend, my dad took me shopping. He helped me find a small, pink purse. I kept my library card in the purse, all by itself. I always took my purse with me when we went to the library, and it made me feel grown-up and important. I loved walking among the stacks of books and sitting in the children's section looking at picture books with Ahddie Mae. By now I was old enough to read real books . . . books without pictures. Checking out books at the end of our library visit was exciting. I was allowed to take three books at a time. I took my library card out of my pink purse and presented it to the librarian.

That summer I read many books, but the one I most remember and loved was *Black Beauty*. It was the first book that took me into a new world. I had no idea that it had been written a hundred years earlier. The horse came alive for me, and I still enjoy reading horse stories to this day: *Flicka*, *Secretariat*, *Lucky*, and *Black Beauty*.

Time with my father was always precious. I wanted that summer to never end. I knew I was a lucky girl.

The Dark Side

My stepfather, Art, came back from Korea in 1953 when the war was ending. I was ten years old and back in California with my mommy for the school year, still living in the projects. When Art first came back, I tiptoed around him, trying to be invisible, not just because he had always treated me badly but because I could feel his eyes on me. I didn't know what was coming, but I knew it was going to be awful.

I was two years older than when he had left. Small breasts had emerged on my chest. One day when I was alone getting dressed in the kid's bedroom, Mommy came in and handed me one of her old bras.

"Here, put this on," she said. "You need to start wearing a bra." It was ugly, raggedy, faded, and discolored from years of use. Two of the three hooks in the back were missing, so it wasn't going to close right. One of the straps had broken and been tied back together in a big knot that would show through my clothing. I hated it.

"I don't need that," I said.

"Yes, you do," she replied. "If you don't wear the bra, people are going to see you jiggling around under your clothes."

I didn't want to need a bra. I wasn't happy about having breasts, either. But Mommy was right. I had to wear the awful bra so people wouldn't see me jiggle. I put it on, and it looked even uglier. It was too tight in some places, too loose in others. I tugged at it, trying to get it to sit right, but it didn't help. No one had warned me that this weird stuff was going to happen . . . body parts changing unexpectedly and awful underwear to hold everything in place.

The only thing worse than the bra was getting my period. When I showed Mommy the blood on the toilet paper she said, "You've had it now."

She didn't say, "You've *got* it, now."

It sounded like it was all over for me when she said, "You've had it." Apparently, the bad part of my life was now starting. My entry into puberty was an unhappy one.

Just like before he went to Korea, Art was once again finding fault with everything I did, even the smallest, most inconsequential things. For example, I had a habit of sitting on my left hand at the dinner table, hanging my arm down with my hand outside my leg, and then tucking my hand between my thigh and the chair. For some reason he would scream at me about it.

"Mary Helen, if I've told you once, I've told you a thousand times to get that damn hand into your lap where it belongs. We don't sit on our hands at the table in this house. You act like some kind of animal who can't behave like a normal person."

The minute he started yelling, I would realize I had once again forgotten about his objection to my sitting this way. I would jerk my hand into my lap as fast as I could.

"I'm sorry," I said. "I forgot."

"You say you forgot, Mary Helen. But you know what I think? I think maybe you enjoy this so called 'forgetting.' You've been told over and over that it's bad behavior, and that's exactly why you do it. You remember perfectly well, don't you? But you do it anyway, don't you?"

This felt so unjust, but I didn't dare contradict him. Then, after a while, even before the meal was over, I would forget again, my hand naturally tucking itself under my thigh. I wasn't even aware of it. Art would catch me again and go into a furious rage.

"This is nothing short of deliberate disobedience, Mary Helen. You are doing your best to get away with this and show everybody how you refuse to cooperate with this family in any way. Get up right now and take your rotten little self out of this room. Don't come back. You haven't earned the right to join the rest of us. I've had it with you. We've all had it with you."

"I'm sorry, I didn't mean it, I forgot." This apology elicited only a sneer from Art. I tried to be invisible, shrinking away from the table, not having had enough to eat, knowing nothing I did was right. How could I have sat on my hand again when I knew how angry he would get?

Mommy was always silent when Art yelled at me. At the table, she kept her eyes on her plate and didn't look up. She knew, and I knew as well, that one word in my defense would start his yelling at her instead of me. He was much more violent with her, and he would probably get physical quickly, grabbing her hair or her arm and pushing her around. I didn't expect her to stick up for me. I knew it would just make things worse. I felt so strongly that all the problems with Art were my fault. If only I could remember not to do the things that made him angry. But I kept forgetting.

That feeling that things were my fault stayed with me day after day. In time, it became a familiar feeling, and eventually, it stayed with me for decades.

It was many years later when I saw what was really at play with Art. He saw me, from the day he met me, as a constant reminder that my mother had been with someone else before him, namely my father. I think this drove him into states of jealousy where he wanted to make me pay.

I had known for years that my mother was not mentally sound. She did crazy things. One time, when I was around two years old, she set the curtains on fire. Another time, when I was older, she forgot the little kids in the bathtub for hours, until they were cold and screaming, which she somehow didn't hear. She was drinking way more than usual.

Her brother, who lived nearby, explained to me that, from time to time, she needed to go away and spend a few weeks in the sanitarium. I didn't know what a sanitarium was, I just knew she went there. This had always been true, and there had always been relatives nearby to take care of us kids while she was gone. In Georgia, it had been her sisters, and recently, in California, her nearby brother and his family. These relatives explained things to me, that Mommy couldn't help it and sometimes she just needed to go away and get better.

But now that Art was back, Mommy had to go away more and more frequently. When Mommy was home, I felt safe. Art wouldn't dare to bother me and risk her finding out. But whenever she was gone, there was nothing to stop him.

Many a night, he would come into the bedroom that I shared with the littler kids. There were three narrow metal beds in the room, no other furniture or lamps or anything on the walls. Our clothes were in cardboard boxes under our beds.

One night, around midnight, Art came in as usual. The two little ones lay asleep in their own beds across the room from me. They slept soundly, but I woke up the minute he came to the door. Even when I slept, I never slept soundly because a part of me was awake watching . . . worried about him coming after me. The moment he loomed in the doorway I was instantly wide awake. I woke up in a panic with my heart racing. I dreaded what I knew was coming. I felt sick to my stomach, a wave of nausea rolling through me.

Art sat down on my bed so close to me that I could feel the heat from his body. He didn't say anything to me, not at any time while he was in the room. His breath was heavy with alcohol. He reached his hands into my torn pajamas, stretching his fingers to find my most private parts. I was still as a corpse. I kept my eyes down, looking at the sheets or the floor, anywhere but at him. I was scared to move. I just let him do what he wanted. He put his hands up under my pajama top and played with my small breasts.

He unzipped his fly. He took my hand and pulled it over onto himself, moving my hand up and down, stroking his penis, which got bigger and stood up on its own. I mechanically went along with whatever he had me do. I had seen my cousin's penis when we were young and played doctor, but it was much smaller than what Art was making me touch.

Once Art was aroused, he would pull off my pajama bottoms and have me sit on him and move up and down until he was finished. I don't remember the first time. I don't remember if it hurt me. I just remember hating it.

This was my introduction to sex. I was an unwilling victim, afraid of him and doing whatever he said to do. I was like a robot. The little kids slept through the whole thing.

Mommy came home a few days later, with no idea of what Art had been doing to me while she was gone. She and Art began to have bad fights, much worse than any fights they had before. One night, we heard them argue and scream. Art dragged Mommy into our bedroom.

"You kids need to understand what happens when you don't do as you're supposed to. I told your mother what to do, but she didn't listen to me, did she?" He slapped her face. She reeled back and lost her balance. Art pushed her and knocked her down onto the floor. She banged her head and cried out in pain. The two little kids began to cry, but we were like statues, afraid to move.

"I told you to eat the fat from the ham, but you refused to eat it, didn't you? You like the fat from other meats, but you just plain refused to eat the fat from the ham. I told you the fat from a ham is the very best tasting fat to eat. But you wouldn't even try a little bit of it. No, not even a single bite. That's the kind of person you are. You just want to make other people angry and upset. Well, it worked, didn't it? And now I have to teach you a lesson. I have to go through all this, and the kids have to go through all this, just because you're stubborn and won't do as you're told."

Mommy was lying face up on the floor. Art sat on top of her, pinning her hands to the floor with both his arms, hate on his face, hateful words streaming from his mouth. Mommy kicked her legs up trying to strike him in the back. She screamed at me, begging, "Mary Helen, go get the scissors and stab him in the back." I was too scared to move, and I definitely wasn't going to stab anyone.

Later that night, I wrote a letter to my father in New York asking him to let me come live with him. I didn't tell him why. I never told anyone else what Art did to me when he came into my bed at night, not until many years later. I was so ashamed of it. I felt everything that happened with Art was my fault. I had caused it by being too nice, or too helpful, or too forgetful, or too obedient. I didn't know how I had caused it, but I had no doubt it was my fault. Eventually, my real father told me I could come to live with him. This was a glimmer of sunlight and warmth after a long winter in the Arctic.

Pinkie
and Blue Boy

Riverdale, the neighborhood where Nana lived, lies on the Hudson River. The train to Grand Central Station runs along the river and takes half an hour. Riverdale includes a small section known as Fieldston, populated with many large multimillion-dollar homes situated on lush acreage. Fieldston is home to the fancy Riverdale Country School, as well as to the Fieldston Ethical Culture School.

I understood Ethical Culture as a kind of non-religion that promoted being a good person. Education at the Fieldston School centered on exploring ethical behavior. When I lived in Riverdale, the Fieldston School was considered so liberal that people called it "Moscow on the Hudson," Moscow's brand of Communism being considered about as liberal as you could get in the early fifties.

In more recent years, many high-rise apartment buildings have been built in less residential parts of Riverdale, mostly undistinguished but good places to live, close to the city and the subway. It's not too far down the hill to get the trains along the river, but it's well removed from the hustle of Manhattan.

In the 1800s, Manhattan moguls had come to Riverdale to build their country estates. Later, around 1915, many smaller homes were added to the neighborhood. At the time, my grandfather, Robert Fein, built a colonial brick house. It was not too large, and it was symmetrical in design. There were white shutters and a tree in the front yard. I remember colorful zinnia bushes on either side of the front door.

Attached to the house was a second lot, a big grassy plot dedicated to lawn chairs. It was bordered at the sidewalk by a boxwood hedge interlaced with honeysuckle vines. These vines, with their fragrant white flowers, were perfect for creating majestic floral crowns and tiaras for me and the other six-year-old girls who came to play.

After my parents divorced, my father moved back into the house with his mother. He was tall with brown eyes and dark hair. He had big shoulders, and I thought he was quite handsome. He had an approachable and friendly look about himself. And he always had a twinkle in his eye for me.

When I was ten years old, he had already been living with his mother for six years. That was the year when he remarried. I was in California and was not invited to the wedding. But I was invited to come and spend a year with his new family.

My father and my new stepmother, Winnie, met me at Idlewild Airport. Winnie was not nearly as pretty as my real mother. She was short, only about five feet tall. Even at ten years old, I was taller than she was. Although she wasn't pretty, she was what she would call "well pulled together," with nice outfits and hair done weekly. She was opinionated, smart, and outspoken, often critical of whatever she thought could be improved. She was practical, and she looked practical. She smiled at me when we first saw one another but only briefly. Winnie had a daughter named Adrienne whom everyone called Rennie. Winnie and Rennie.

Rennie had also come to the airport to greet me. She was

six years old, four years younger than I. She was a beautiful child, delicate, with an open face and straight brown hair that fell like silk when she bent down. Her eyes were gentle blue, and she always had a sweet and quiet manner. I was charmed by her lovely presence, and so were all the adults in her life. Rennie looked like an enchanted fairy girl from a storybook.

Before marrying my dad, Winnie and Rennie lived with Winnie's mother Guinevere. Guinevere had spent thirty years in her elegant stone house in Fieldston. Winnie had grown up with every luxury. She went to good schools, ate meals prepared by the household's own professional cook, and was chauffeured about by a full-time driver.

Once she and my dad married, they moved into an apartment in Riverdale Park, a nearby apartment complex. Three of my father's siblings lived in Riverdale Park, moving there after they married and starting their own families. All my aunts, uncles, and cousins were within walking distance, and all were close to Nana still living in the original family home.

Rennie and I shared the apartment's larger bedroom, and the parents took the small one. Rennie looked up to me in a way that I liked very much. It was a pleasant first for me. But I was also jealous of Rennie. She had a closet full of toys, and I had no toys, having brought only one small suitcase of practical clothing from California. I remember counting every single toy she had, and then announcing to our parents that I had four toys and Rennie had one hundred and twenty-eight. I don't remember any positive results from this. I just remember feeling jealous.

Winnie gave me books to read, taught me to play piano and read music, and helped me understand politics as we saw it on TV, as much as a ten-year-old needed or cared to. My world began to open up.

Pinkie and Blue Boy

Riverdale Park had four apartments on a floor, so we would often see our neighbors on the elevator. Whatever anyone was cooking for dinner would waft its aroma across the entire fifth floor. Each apartment had a large living room, big enough for a grand piano. There were lots of windows looking out over surrounding lawns and sky. The kitchen was tiny, with just enough room to open the refrigerator door and only about two feet of counter space. A wide hallway doubled as a dining room. But it was a very nice place to live. I loved Riverdale Park.

My playmates were my first cousins, Deborah and Barbara Fein, the three of us born in the same year to three of the six Fein brothers. Deborah was only a few months older than me, but she was a full grade ahead of me. I admired her and hoped I could be more like her. She had confidence. She had long hair and was a thin person, something I devoutly wished I were. Barbara was just a little younger than me, not dynamic like Deborah, but sweet and good to be with. We were a happy threesome, the first cousins.

After dinner, every night all summer, we were allowed to go outside and play on the sidewalks. Riverdale Park had little traffic. Wide sidewalks provided safety and plenty of room for our small group of five or six girls. We had a variety of important things to accomplish each evening.

Leaning on cars was our first group activity, kind of a warm-up. It was comfortable and conducive to conversation. Cars were parked on both sides of the narrow streets that ran through Riverdale Park. Half of our group would lean on the cars parked on one side of the street. We could then easily converse with the other half of our group, leaning on cars on the opposite side, only about one car width away. As soon as enough kids showed up, we began our games: hopscotch, jump rope, and a number of games played with a pink rubber ball.

Moments of Knowing

In our neighborhood, every kid knew the Good Humor ice cream truck would be coming down the street sometime after dinner. The arrival of the Good Humor Man in his white truck was the major event of the evening. The first sign of the truck was its musical jingle. The song played by Good Humor trucks everywhere in the 1950s was, "Turkey in the Straw."

Even today, when I hear "Turkey in the Straw," I want an ice cream.

The song was later discovered to have racist roots. In the 1800s, it was played in minstrel shows where actors wore blackface and acted out racist stereotypes. Thus, in 2020 (long after our time), "Turkey in the Straw" was abandoned by Good Humor in favor of a new jingle by RZA, founder of the Staten Island hip-hop collective Wu-Tang Clan. It's actually kind of catchy.

But to us children, unaware of its ugly origins, the sound of "Turkey in the Straw" meant ice cream, glorious ice cream. What could be better on a summer night? My family lived on the fifth floor, so I always brought my quarter down with me. My favorite Good Humor was a "Toasted Almond." This delicious concoction was vanilla ice cream served on a stick and covered all over with golden bits of crushed almond.

We pronounced "Good Humor Man" as "Gudchuma Man." Some kids lived on the lower floors of the apartment buildings, and when the ice cream truck came by, they could stand beneath their apartment windows and holler up, "Hey Mom, the Gudchuma man's here. Throw down a quarter!" One girl didn't like ice cream, so she would holler, "Hey Mom, the Gudchuma man's here. Throw down a lemon."

After ice cream, we would start our pink rubber ball games. Many of us had a ball with "Spalding" written on it in script. The ball was about two and a half inches in diameter. We called it a "Spaldeen."

Pinkie and Blue Boy

There were lots of great games to play with a Spaldeen. "A, my name is Alice" was a favorite. You bounced the ball and you had to throw your leg over the ball frequently. "B, my name is Betty," all the way up to "Z, my name is Zoey."

Another game with a Spaldeen was 7-Up. You bounced the pink ball against a wall and performed specific skills between bounces. Throw the ball at the wall, clap once. Throw again and clap twice, then three times, etc., until you missed the ball because you were busy clapping. There was also jumping in the air before catching the ball. Throw, jump once, throw, jump twice, etc.

The activity I loved above all else was trading cards. At the height of my card trading career, I had a stack of cards about four inches high. I was quite proud of this enormous collection, dog-eared from constant handling, my pride and joy. I could barely hold them all in one hand.

The trading cards we collected were not like boys' baseball cards . . . not sports related. I think they started out as single cards culled from actual decks of grown-up playing cards that had a pretty picture on the back. But by the time we were collecting them, trading cards were for sale in the toy and party store. The ones we bought were just blank white on the back. The important part of a trading card was the picture on the front.

Everyone organized their stack of trading cards by category. Some important trading card categories were Pin-Ups, Animals, Sports, Flowers, Boats (mostly tall ships at sea in full sail), and Western Scenes (mountains, lakes, waterfalls). There was a Car category and a Movie Star category, with stars like Shirley Temple and Marilyn Monroe.

My favorite category was the one with cards depicting famous paintings. The category was called Famouses. The Mona Lisa was the most valuable card in the category. My most highly prized Famous category cards were Pinkie and Blue Boy. A while earlier, I had traded someone to get Pinkie. Then I waited for months until one day I finally traded to get Blue Boy. This was a wonderful day in my young life when I was able to unite Pinkie and Blue Boy.

Blue Boy was a well-known Thomas Gainsborough painting of a young boy dressed in blue satin. Gainsborough painted it in 1770. The boy stands before a rustic landscape in earth tones. He holds his hat with a large, white feather down by his side, and he has bows on his shoes.

Pinkie was painted in 1794 by a different artist, Sir Thomas Lawrence. Pinkie was a lovely young girl. She wears a pale, pink dress with a pink satin cummerbund. She has a matching hat from which two long ties gracefully blow in a light breeze. Pinkie is set against a light sky.

Of course, the ten-year-old me didn't know any of this or care. What mattered was that this girl Pinkie was simply made in heaven to be with this Blue Boy. When seen side by side, one would think that they had been painted as a pair. But Gainsborough and Lawrence were far from collaborators. In fact, they were fierce competitors. They would have been shocked at the thought that their fine creations would be joined in the future.

In the 1920s, American railroad magnate Henry E. Huntington purchased the two paintings and hung them side by side in his mansion, today part of the Huntington Hartford Museum in Pasadena, California. The two paintings still hang there today. By two different artists, painted twenty-five years apart, and depicting subjects who would have lived 150 years apart, this pair is a perfect set. One writer called them the "Romeo and Juliet of portraiture."

Most of the girls in our group had respectable trading card collections. Whenever I wanted to get rid of some cards, I would make a special pile and then find someone who wanted to trade for some new cards. We'd both stand. I would reveal the top card in my get-rid-of pile, and the other kid would say either, "Got it," or "Need it." Then I threw that card onto the ground into either the "got it" pile or the "need it" pile. As we went through the cards, the soundtrack went faster.

"Got it, got it, need it, got it."

Once we had worked through all the cards, we reviewed the "need it" pile together and negotiated. A card I valued greatly would trade for several of the other kid's good cards. Somehow, we all knew the value of each card, and we worked out a fair trade. I must have traded a number of valuable cards to get Pinkie and Blue Boy.

Last Days in California

After spending a year in Riverdale with my dad and Winnie, I was sent back to my mother in California. I think it was because Winnie and I didn't get along that well. Despite the many doors she opened for me, we had our difficulties.

Once again, I hated being in the projects, and once again I begged my father to let me come to live with them. But I spent another year in California before he said yes. I hated the projects. It seemed to me that half the men and boys I came across wanted to molest me: my stepfather Art, adult neighbors, older boys. Not only were there sexual threats, there was also the threat of violence. I was scared of someone breaking in while my mother was away at work. There were always loud noises and screams in the night. I never felt safe in Carmelites.

I caught something called "trench mouth." It's a rare disease in the United States caused by a lack of dental hygiene. I didn't even have a toothbrush, and I had never been to a dentist. My mother didn't have money for that kind of luxury. I lay on the couch with a high fever for two weeks.

One day while I was sick, my mother brought in a friend of hers who was known to all the neighbors as a "health food nut."

Last Days in California

Today, she would be admired for her eating habits but not back then. She was unattractive woman with a harsh tone of voice. She told me she was going to get rid of "this problem of mine." Her hair was tangled and hardly looked combed, and her face had several red sores. I didn't want to be near her.

She brought over a bowl of a strange, white, creamy substance called "yogurt."

"This is going to make you all better right away," she said, crouching down next to me with her bowl and spoon. She lifted a spoonful of her miracle cure to my mouth. I had no choice but to open wide and take in the awful substance.

"Isn't that wonderful!" my mother said supportively, "My friend has brought something that is going to fix you right up!"

She continued to spoon the miracle cure into my mouth leaving me no choice but to swallow it all. I don't think I even tasted it; I just reacted to it being strange and slimy and unknown. This was yogurt in the mid-fifties, a little-known substance for medicinal purposes only. Who could imagine that in sixty years it would take up a whole wall of every supermarket and half a shelf in my own refrigerator.

After a week or two, I recovered from having trench mouth, despite the yogurt treatment having no effect. There were no long-term effects from the sickness. I still didn't get a toothbrush or see a dentist until I moved to New York where such things were the new normal.

I had a boyfriend for a while. His name was John Davis, and when we first were getting to know one another, he was very nice to me, always stopping to talk with me when we met outside. He lived only one building away. I thought he was good-looking and friendly. He was bigger than me, which I liked because I had already gotten taller than most of the girls my age and even some of the boys. Being taller than a boy seemed unfeminine to me, so I hated being tall. Being tall and overweight made things even worse because that meant I was just plain big. I hated being big.

John tried to kiss me a few times, but I turned away, not interested. But he didn't seem to mind, and he continued to be fun and was always pleasant.

Everything changed when he learned I was leaving for New York. The night before I left, he asked me to come visit him. I could tell as soon as I entered the house that he was not the person I was used to. No one else was home. He grabbed me and kissed me roughly as I entered, reaching out with one hand to close and lock the door as he pulled me onto the couch. He put his hands up under my blouse and tried to reach down into my pants. I wriggled away from his grabbiness, since I knew that his plan was to force me to have sex with him.

Thanks to Art, I knew what sex was, and I knew I wasn't interested. But there I was sitting on his lap as he pawed over me. He pulled a photograph out of his pocket to show me. It was my mother, naked and standing up facing the camera. She was holding a big bunch of roses just below her breasts and giving a come-hither look. I was shocked. I had never imagined anything like this photo might exist. I felt like my mother was a whore.

"I'm going to show this to everyone if you don't do what I want." I thought about this and realized I would be gone the next day and he probably wouldn't bother. I decided to run.

I was thinking, scheming about how I could distract him and get away. I managed to position myself so that I was closer to the door than he was. I considered the exact moves I would need. I would have to lull him into a sense of security, a relaxed state where he was sure it was all going his way. Then I would have to leap up and reach the door before him, with enough time to unlock the door fast, without a fumble, and then fly out of the house. I was one thousand percent determined to pull it off and save myself.

I let him paw me a bit, pretending to relax on his lap and enjoy his rough attention. I could tell he was getting into it and forgetting about restraining me. Then, at just the right moment, before he could even realize what was happening, I jumped up, threw the lock, and ran out the door. I had to use every bit of my wits to escape. I can still hear the sound and feel the tapping of my feet running away from him, down the sidewalk, toward home. All these years later, I still remember every detail and thought and sound from that experience when I was twelve.

The next day I flew to New York. My mother took me to the airport. She was drinking more lately and being a lot less predictable. Saying goodbye at the airport was the last time I would ever see her.

Scarsdale

Finally, my father had said yes to me moving back East to live with him, Winnie, and Rennie. I was so happy. I was ready to get on with my new life and leave the rough past behind.

The family had moved from Riverdale to the town of Scarsdale in Westchester County, north of New York City. Scarsdale is one of the most affluent communities in the United States. That was true when I first arrived there in 1955, and it is still true today. It's a beautiful suburb, leafy and green with many stately homes. Most of the larger houses were built in the early 1900s. The house we lived in was a more modest, upper middle-class house, in a neighborhood built in the 1930s. Scarsdale has a certain notoriety in the New York area, known for being home to the rich and the very rich.

Unlike my previous visit East, this time it was understood I would stay permanently. Marvin and Winnie had moved to Scarsdale for the excellent school system, and they wanted me to benefit from this. Scarsdale schools had the highest academic ratings possible. School here was challenging and kept my interest.

The town was completely residential except for a small commercial area of four or five blocks designed to look like a Tudor village. It's only eighteen miles from Manhattan, less than an hour to Grand Central Station by commuter train. This made it an ideal place for those who worked in the city but wanted to live in a beautiful town.

I didn't know we were wealthy. But gradually I figured it out.

I had new clothes for the first time in my life. My stepmother threw out my frayed and stained old things from California. She took me to the cheapest store in the town of White Plains. That was where people shopped if they lived in Scarsdale. She bought her clothes and her daughter's clothes at Bergdorf's and Sax Fifth Avenue. But I was happy to have any kind of new clothes for the first time in my life, even if they were from Alexander's or Klein's on the Square.

Every day, my new clothes were clean and ironed when I put them on in the morning. Winnie had a maid who came one day a week just to do the laundry and ironing. She had a different maid on a different day to clean the house. For the first time, I wore clothes that weren't torn or faded or too small. I knew they weren't as good as Winnie's and Rennie's clothes, and I knew I was the maybe-welcomed-maybe-not stepdaughter in the house. But I loved the new clothes.

Our house in Scarsdale was a two-story house, gray clapboard, with black shutters . . . colonial, symmetrical, welcoming. The house sat back from the street on a green lawn surrounded by well-groomed hedges. The rest of the family had moved in a few months before I arrived, but my room was ready for me. It was the small room in the middle of the upstairs, and they had asked me by phone what color to paint it.

"Please," I said, "green." I was delighted when I arrived to see the perfect pale green.

One side of my room had a slanted wall, which I loved. I had never had my own room before, and now I even had two windows looking out over the large backyard. I could see a playhouse and a small fishpond. There were flowers and fruit trees.

In the Long Beach projects, we had lived in an undecorated concrete box, strung together with five other identical concrete boxes to make one long building for six families. Our building for six families was surrounded by dozens of buildings exactly the same as ours. There were parking lots and more buildings and more groups of buildings. All the same concrete boxes.

Our home, like all the other concrete boxes, had two concrete rooms downstairs and two concrete rooms upstairs with a bathroom. My mother had one of the upstairs rooms, and we three children shared the other bedroom, three narrow beds filling all the space. Mommy needed privacy because men came by. She had a couple of boyfriends, and they were nice enough to us. No child molesters. At least there was that.

One day I forgot to knock first, and I walked in on her with one of the boyfriends. I saw a fast flash with lots of pink flesh. In a moment, I realized they were naked, having sex on the bed. I turned around and ran into the bathroom. My mother jumped up and followed me, angry, her features distorted. She yelled at me and slapped me across the face.

This had been another moment that had driven me to beg my dad to let me come and live with him.

Scarsdale was safe. There were no visiting boyfriends, and no grownups having sex in the next room. No rough characters lurking around outside. No concrete boxes anywhere. Just a beautiful house on a beautiful street.

I was in a fuzzy daze for the first several years in Scarsdale. Moving and changing everything about my life seemed to shock my entire system. It was good to be in a quiet town without violence. But I had no idea how anything worked. My world grew fuzzy, and nothing really got to me through the fuzz.

Scarsdale

I entered seventh grade in Scarsdale. The school immediately put me in remedial reading. I knew this was wrong because I had always been the best reader in the class, ever since first grade. Winnie seemed to take this as a personal insult because she came to the school immediately and put up a fuss. Soon I was back in regular English class. Winnie fought for me.

The classes were wonderful. They held my interest and took me on journeys. I visited new worlds, like the stock market. In math class, we each chose a stock to pretend to buy. Every day, we looked up our stock in the *New York Times*. The print was tiny, but I was thrilled to track my make-believe financial progress.

My uncle Ernie, my dad's black sheep, merchant marine brother whom I adored, had always played the market. He gave me a hot tip. On his advice, I pretend-bought stock in a new company called Litton Industries. The teacher was upset because she did not approve of stocks being bought on the little board—the American Stock Exchange. We were supposed to buy only from the big board, the New York Stock Exchange. My stock was traded on the little board, the second largest exchange in the United States. But not good enough for my math teacher. At Scarsdale High School, we were trained to pick only the best of everything.

During the three weeks of our math class experiment, my stock increased tenfold. I made more pretend money than anyone else in the class. Although this did not endear me to the teacher, it made me very happy. Success at school was rare for me. Generally, I felt left out and unpopular. I made one or two good friends, girlfriends on my street. I had fun with them, and they accepted me as I was. But, overall, I was not very happy socially at Scarsdale High School.

The next year, when I was thirteen, my mother died. I

felt sad and guilty. And I felt overwhelmingly hungry. I never realized the hunger started with her death until many years later, but it did. Before she died, I weighed 128 pounds. Not overweight, but just right and normal for my height. After her death, I gained ten pounds a year for the next six years. By the time I graduated from high school, I was nearing two hundred pounds.

In high school social circles, being overweight was a fatal strike against acceptance. Today, in more diversity-aware circles, there is finally an effort to understand and to accept, to question why fat is seen as ugly in our culture but beautiful in others, to question the cruelty that an overweight person elicits. But not then.

I lived in my fuzzy daze. One day, a certain neighbor boy and I were the only ones getting off the school bus at the corner near where I lived. Buses to my neighborhood left the school several times each afternoon, and on that day, I had taken a late bus. The usual girls from my block had all taken earlier buses, so the boy and I were the only ones getting off. We were alone on this corner with no one else around. I turned to walk home, but he walked after me, even though he lived in a different direction.

"I want to talk to you," he said. I turned around to face him. He walked up too close to me, and then he reached up with both hands and grabbed my breasts. "Doesn't that feel good," he leered.

It did not feel good, and I was frightened. I wanted to slap his hands away, but I was too afraid to do anything. I remembered the boys from the projects, who threatened to hit me. I was afraid this boy would do the same. I just stood there until he got tired of squeezing my breasts. He turned away without a word and headed for home. I stood there frozen. Finally, I walked home. I never let myself be anywhere near that boy again. I would get off the bus at a different stop and walk a long way to get home before I would take a chance getting off at the same stop as him.

Other boys were interested in me. I didn't resist. I was easy. As long as they pretended to be interested in me for who I was. As long as they kept up an illusion of courtship and respect for at least the first hour. As long as there was no violence.

I only remember one scene vividly, but I know there were others. I was out on the football field at night on the dark edges of a party with a boy named Steven. Steven was popular and never spoke to me before or after this incident. He had wandered over to me and struck up a conversation. I could see he was looking at my breasts while I was talking and not listening to what I was saying, so I knew why he had stopped to talk to me.

Soon, with little ceremony, I was lying under him as he rubbed himself against me. Our clothes were on, but I felt awful about myself. I felt like I was some kind of whore, a person with no morals who would lay down with this boy who wouldn't even speak to me and then would let him touch me. But there was his attention, and it didn't matter how I got it. At least he was concentrating on me and me alone. My high school years were studded with unpleasant sexual incidents.

My dad was busy at work often. He was an electrical engineer, and he worked as a salesman for General Electric in New York City. His specialty was equipment that detected and prevented power outages. While he was busy with his work, Winnie, Rennie, and I were home together most afternoons. It was not usually a fun time with them. Apparently, I was difficult. I didn't know that dirty laundry shouldn't go back into the drawers with the clean stuff. I didn't get the dishes clean enough when I washed them. I didn't know how to set the table right. All that was hard for Winnie. Eventually she taught me.

One day, there was a moment that I remember very clearly. We were in the kitchen, and Winnie was angry at me. Then, she took it out on my father. She said that he preferred me to her, like I was a rival, trying to be my father's girlfriend. I thought she was crazy. But when she made this accusation, I realized she wasn't all in one piece, either. Like me. That made me feel sorry for her, and it made me like her a little more, in spite of her crazy remark.

Our family of four had some good moments. One day we were driving along the Bronx River Parkway, my dad behind the wheel and Winnie in the front seat. The two of us kids were in the back. A song we had never heard came on the radio . . . something about a lonely street and a place called Heartbreak Hotel. None of us had ever heard anything like it before. My dad pulled the car off the road and stopped on the grassy edge until the song ended. He was tapping his hand on the steering wheel. The four of us had heard Elvis for the very first time.

While Rennie had been a beautiful six-year-old when I first arrived in New York, within the next five years she gained a great deal of weight and became angry most of the time. I don't know why. Maybe it was having to share her mother with my father and me. Maybe it was that her own father had walked out when she was young. Winnie told me that one time they ran into him on the streets of New York, but he took one look at his daughter and turned and walked away. Rennie recognized him and started to cry when he ignored them. A haunting scene.

Whatever it was, her childhood beauty never returned. Her constant anger changed her. Instead of being a lovely and inno-cent presence, she was now unpleasant to have around. She spent most of her free time reading in her room with the door shut. She was not someone most people even wanted to have a conversation with.

She did develop a circle of friends when she was in high school. Rennie loved science fiction. She met Arthur at a science fiction convention in New York, and he became her boyfriend. Together they added several friends to a circle of fans, all of whom went to science fiction conventions together around the country. This was a wonderful improvement in her life.

Rennie wrote one of the few fanzines of the 1960s. A fanzine is a science fiction magazine for the most avid sci-fi fans. Rennie called it Feinzine, and it was apparently quite well-known in the sci-fi world.

Rennie died young at the age of 36. She loved to feed the fish at the duck pond in Scarsdale. One day she fell there and broke her leg. She needed surgery to fix it, but once she was admitted to the hospital, they discovered she had late-stage ovarian cancer and a very short time to live. I visited her in the hospital and brought her a beautiful red silk scarf that she loved. I have it today and think of her whenever I see it. Within a few days of my visit, she had died.

Winnie was devastated. She asked Rennie's sci-fi friends to go to her apartment and take anything they wanted. They were kind enough to empty out the apartment and return the keys to the owner.

I kept a diary, but I knew Winnie would find it and read it, so I kept it in code. I don't know how I learned the code I used. It's called the Tic Tac Toe code or the Pigpen Cipher. It was a simple geometric substitution cipher, exchanging letters for symbols.

Later in life I researched the code, hoping to figure out how I had discovered it. It turned out to be a Rosicrucian cypher invented hundreds of years ago. It had been used by a number of secret organizations, such as the Order of the Golden Dawn. When I was a kid, I didn't know any of this history, but I was thrilled as I wrote pages of incomprehensible symbols that only I could understand. I never remembered how I found the code, but I never forgot how to decode it.

Our house in Scarsdale was at the top of a long hill. There were about ten houses on either side of the street. Eight girls who were all in my grade at school lived on our block. The eight of us waited for the school bus together every morning. We all wore white bobby socks and brown-and-white oxfords. The best outfit was a straight skirt, with a cashmere cardigan that had a grosgrain ribbon down the front for the buttons. But I was too fat for straight skirts, and Winnie wasn't buying me cashmere. Still, the eight of us were all nice to one another because we lived on the same block.

I was the first girl to have tights. Winnie had an adventurous side, and one day she came home with the world's first pairs of tights, a pair for each of us. Mine were red. Tights were a new thing in the fifties. Before then, it had been stockings and a garter belt or a girdle—serious torture devices. Tights were great because they came all the way up to the waist and no uncomfortable metal hardware was needed to keep them up. I remember lifting my skirt in girls' choir so that everyone could see my new tights. Everyone loved them. Tights were clearly the future.

I still love them today.

~

I had a good voice, and I loved to sing. I was accepted into the school's choir for girls, called the Choralettes. We met for an hour, five mornings a week, starting at 8:30. There were about twenty of us, and we had the best voices in the school. I loved being in the Choralettes. Getting in was competitive, and I was thrilled and proud to belong. It was the most important part of my life.

I gave my life over to music. Whenever someone asked what I wanted to be when I grew up, I always replied, "An opera singer." I didn't know anything about opera, but I knew that was a kind of singer I might become. Music was another world I could go to. Singing took me on soaring emotional journeys such as I had never imagined. When our girls' choir sang, our voices blended into a unique beauty. Being part of that sound was a joy.

We were constantly told by our music teacher, Mr. Walter Ehret, that we were the "best girls' choir in America." Mr. Ehret was a wonderful teacher who inspired us all. We were his pride and joy. Nothing in my own life was as important as the Choralettes. All the girls in the group became friends, traveling together on wings of song, all devoted to our group and to our teacher. We gave a few concerts at the school each year. One year, I had a solo, singing a song that I loved, "You'll Never Walk Alone," from the Broadway musical *Carousel*. The night of my solo was the height of my young life. A mean boy working the curtain onstage told me I was off-key, which ruined things a little. But mostly I was still thrilled to have been chosen.

The Choralettes cut a record in my senior year, and along with everything else from those years, I lost my copy. Recently, fifty years later, I went to Amazon on a whim and searched for it. It was hard to believe, but there was the Choralettes record for $50.00. I bought it and listened to it and agreed with my former self. We were a wonderful choir. When Mr. Ehret died, I sent his family a thank-you letter explaining how deeply he had enriched my life.

Rich Girl,
Poor Girl

I was happy to be living in the same house with my father. Every day, he put on his hat and his camel's hair coat and rode the commuter train into Manhattan to work. However, the parent I spent the most time with was Winnie.

Winnie had a vibrant side. She was always excitedly interested in something. One year she spent all her time working to get her hero JFK elected president. Another time, she spent a month or two sitting on the back porch in a lawn chair solving a puzzle, a little plastic hand-held game called Hi-Q. She could not get enough of it.

Life was fun for Winnie. She wasn't beautiful, and she didn't care much about appearances. She dressed well and knew how to get done up very nicely for a big event. But in general, she preferred being practical in her dress and in everything else as well.

Her parents were fabulously wealthy. They were Jewish and from Riverdale, just like my father's family. Winnie's father had been successful in the New York garment industry. Winnie wanted for nothing. She attended the best private schools New York had to offer and received a college education at one of the Seven Sister colleges. She was blessed with a keen mind and widespread interests: reading, painting, calligraphy, music, and politics.

I continued at the same school in Scarsdale for six years, straight through to twelfth-grade graduation. I loved the school for its many good points. I was charmed by the old brick school building and the double hung windows in every classroom so high that each room had its own long pole with an iron hook to raise and lower the upper window. There were eight-foot-wide polished wooden staircases that we climbed between classes. Lawns and landscaping surrounded the building. No more dusty, temporary California school buildings surrounded by nothing but treeless asphalt.

Teachers were smart and for the most part were very good at making classes interesting. I loved English class, especially in eleventh grade with Mr. Withers. He assigned us to read Emerson's "Self-Reliance," a life changing essay for me. One day the homework he gave us was to write an essay called "The Secrets of My Bottom Drawer." I was ready for that, even if it wasn't just the bottom drawer. For the first time I began to think of writing as something I loved doing. Maybe not just for myself.

At home, I was getting to know my new family better. I enjoyed Rennie for her good mind, and it was fun to be together. I became fond of her, in part because I saw she was so often suffering.

There were many strange things that went on at home. Winnie and Rennie were very close to one another. They would cuddle in bed together for hours with the door closed. This mystified me, but it was just one more incomprehensible thing in my new incomprehensible world. Now I can see that this was about comforting one another. Life was not easy for Rennie. Today, Rennie would be diagnosed as autistic, but we didn't even know that word in 1955. Everyone who met Rennie simply found her to be annoying. She had a whiny voice and was never short on complaints. She had no social skills. Somehow, that part of her development had not happened. She was overweight, like me. We shared that social kiss of death.

Nothing was easy for Rennie if other people were involved. School was a nightmare because she was almost universally rejected by her classmates. She lived in emotional pain every day. The cuddling with her mother was about making up for how difficult her days were.

I learned to love her despite how hard it was to be around her. She was smart, and she admired me. No one had ever looked up to me before, and I was flattered by her admiration. She probably looked up to me because I was four years older and also because I had a friend or two, which she did not.

I did love her in return. She was razor smart. She read only science fiction and couldn't talk much about it, but I marveled from afar at her reading. She had a good sense of humor when she was calm enough to enjoy herself. There was a shy person inside who wanted to understand more about others.

We had fun together. We discovered a secret language, kind of like Pig Latin, another language popular with kids at that time. Our language was called, "Ahby Dahby." We called it "Ob," and enjoyed having discussions at the dinner table that our parents couldn't understand. They were usually short discussions.

"Cahban yahbou spahbeak Ahby Dahby?"

Winnie and Rennie loved animals. I had never had a pet before, but I quickly learned to love them. A rabbit named Hey-You-Stop-Biting-My-Fingers lived in the garage. We had a shy Shetland sheep dog, a tricolor named Sheppy. He had a slight limp and had been the runt of the litter. The family had taken a whole day and driven out to the country to a farm where we could pick out a dog. From the moment we saw Sheppy, we all adored him.

Our menagerie included an entire family of Siamese cats. The mother was a pale blue point named Wendy, and the father a big dark seal point named Caesar. We called him Beany because Caesar was a little too regal for an everyday name. Wendy and Beany had five kittens, who stayed forever. We were supposed to give them away, but we could not part with them.

Rennie had a parakeet in her room named Pretty-Bird. The bird trainer taught us all to say Pert Tee Bi Urd slowly, over and over in a nice, encouraging tone of voice. We all did that, and after a few months the bird spoke back the same words, fast and chirpy, Pretty Bird!

I had two little turtles named Christopher and Columbus, but they didn't live long. Rennie and I held a formal burial service for them with aluminum foil caskets gently buried in a backyard flower bed.

Winnie taught me to read music and play piano. She gave me interesting books to read, considering I was only twelve. The first book she gave me was Ayn Rand's, *The Fountainhead*. This was a great read for a young person discovering the world, filled with heroes and heroines making a difference and easy to identify with. I didn't realize the conservative and egoistic principles that underlay Ayn Rand's stories. It took me years to get over her philosophy and return to a more generous and compassionate value system. Winnie did not mean for this side effect to happen; she was only wanting to help me discover the joy of reading.

Like many Jewish people who lived in New York, Winnie held and practiced strong liberal values. She cared for people of color and for those who had less than we did. She exerted an open-mindedness and a kind influence over me by how she lived. For that I will always be grateful.

Moments of Knowing

Another book offering from Winnie was Doris Lessing's, *The Golden Notebook*. I loved reading it and went on to read all Lessing's books. Thanks to Winnie, I became a reader, and I haven't been a day without a book for the rest of my life.

Winne and Rennie did a lot of painting. I liked watching them but assumed I could never be any good at it. Music and books were enough for me. I wrote poetry. I kept a diary full of prose and poetry, and I continued recording my most secret thoughts about everything.

Winnie tried hard, but she was not a natural homemaker or nurturing mother. For example, she was a terrible cook. Each night Rennie and I set the table while she cooked. We gave each person a glass of skim milk, a serving of frozen vegetables briefly boiled in water, and a broiled piece of meat or chicken with no enhancements.

In spite of Winnie's imposition of this Spartan diet, I got fatter and fatter. The more boring the food she made for us, the more I was sneaking "bad" food whenever no one was around to catch me. Bread and butter, mayonnaise, cheese, cookies. I was into everything. And as much of it as possible. But no matter how much I ate, it never filled the empty place inside. I had my poetry, and I had my singing. They saved me.

Our high school literary magazine was called *The Jabberwocky*, and the school yearbook was called *The Bandersnatch*. All graduates of Scarsdale High School knew these two fictional creatures from Lewis Carroll's 1871 novel, *Through the Looking-Glass*. It was good that our school publications paid homage to this wonderful writer and his fantasy characters.

In 1960, in my junior year of high school when I was sixteen,

Rich Girl, Poor Girl

The Jabberwocky accepted and printed one of my poems. I was stunned. I was so deeply thrilled that I can still feel it now. It was the first time in my life that I had been recognized by my peers in a positive way for something I loved doing. It was even better than making imaginary money in the stock market.

I can't remember my poem, and I don't have a copy. It was metaphysical, and it started, "Somewhere in the vast expanse of time and space . . ." I forget the rest, but I know it was very profound, as only a sixteen-year-old can be.

My life with my dad, Winnie, and Rennie introduced me to reading, music, and painting, not just to the appreciation of these art forms, but to the idea that people I knew could do these things . . . that even I might do these things.

There were moments of knowing. How are these moments related to the moment of knowing from when I was only five when my kindergarten classmate, Marilyn Cloud, was so unkind on the playground? How are these moments related to the vow I took to live for love? How is creativity related to living for love? Here's what I think.

Every moment we spend creatively, letting the mystery and the flow pass through us without getting in the way with hangups or worries, that's enlightenment. It's being in a state of love, being with things as they are, and not letting preferences or judgments or preconceptions run the show.

Being in the here and now is what allows us to make wonderful art, in all its forms. It's the same with love. We feel love in the here and now. When we step into a moment of love, we naturally feel kindness and friendliness toward those close by and those we don't even know, and even toward those who are unkind, like poor Marilyn Cloud. Today, I imagine her as a kind old lady, of my own age, who looks back on her own early cruelty and suffering with compassion.

Moments of Knowing

When I am in the here and now, I know that every other person is the same as me. Connected to me. For each of us, when we are in the here and now, it especially means that we can feel compassion for those who are suffering, like my autistic stepsister. It means opening the heart until it can hold more than we ever expected. And it means bringing all that into paint or into song or a paragraph.

It's the opening heart that lets creativity happen, lets music come out, lets artwork drop off the brush into the perfect shade and shape, and lets words scratch across the paper with truth.

My Mother Dies

The phone rang after dinner one night. It had been about a year since I had left my mother and moved to live permanently with my dad and Winnie. When that phone rang, it was the first and only time in my life that I knew for sure what was coming next. Somehow, I knew my mother had died, even before my dad and Winnie closed the door to speak privately with the caller and then went upstairs and closed that door, too. They let me watch an extra hour of TV, which they had never done before. After a time, they came back downstairs and called me into the living room. They told me that my mother had driven off a bridge and died.

I knew I hadn't been good to her, not good enough. I hadn't written enough letters to her, telling her about my new life and that I missed her. One letter every few weeks didn't feel nearly sufficient to let her know I loved her and would never turn my back on her. My moving away from her had ended the child support money that my father had sent each month. I knew she never had enough money, and then there had been even less.

I never should have left her. I knew she was driving that broken-down old Ford jalopy that was at least ten years old. It probably was the reason she drove off the bridge. Or maybe it was drinking, which was getting worse and worse and could not have helped her driving.

Once I left, there was no one around to watch out for her, to make sure she didn't do things that were too crazy, things that might cause harm to herself or to the little kids. Not that she would ever harm them on purpose, but she didn't always foresee the consequences of her actions. I knew she was unstable. I knew she had set the curtains on fire, and that she had to go away to the sanitarium at least a couple of times a year.

I hadn't been good enough to her, and now she was gone. Cause and effect. At thirteen, I was still young enough to think everything that happened was my fault. It took me years to come out from under the cloud of guilt over her death. I remembered when my "boyfriend" had shown me the naked photo of her, and how he had threatened to show it to all the neighbors. Did he do that? If he did, it would have pushed her over the edge. At least she never knew about my being molested by Art. Thank god for that.

My mother had dark moods. Being around her was often difficult. Sometimes she was fun, loving, and wonderful, but more often she was angry, critical, or simply distracted. Her life was hard. There were the two small children to take care of and support. Much of the time, she was stressed, running out the door to work, racing home to take care of the kids, broke because her bookkeeping job did not pay well. Life was too much.

Her death left a hole in the middle of me. I didn't know it at the time but looking back, I can see it now. I tried all kinds of ways to fill up the emptiness. Food. Boys. Nothing worked.

For years to come I would run from it, moving fast, finding adventures, always something new. Always something exciting enough to keep my attention off what was driving me. I never gave myself the option of down time, time to think, time to review and consider and wonder. I needed to go fast and to stay away from dangerous memories.

I didn't realize these patterns would rule my life as I got older, keeping me away from what I needed to see but could not face: my belief that I had left my mother to die; my shame over somehow causing men to want to touch me and molest me; my worry that I wouldn't measure up in my new community and my new school.

In time, after her death, life settled. I tried to be loving and good to the people around me. I wanted to be thin and pretty, but those dreams were not to be. As soon as my mother died, I began gaining weight. I had no idea why. I saw it as something that was "happening to me." I never thought of it as something caused by my life experiences. And it never seemed to be in my control, no matter what I tried.

I didn't understand how I was driven by conflicts I didn't even know I had, for another example, feeling that Art's molesting me was my own fault. I needed to keep it a secret from everyone. When my mother died, I thought it was my punishment for what had happened with Art.

I had simply left her behind. I was living a new life of luxury with my father. I had new clothes and my own room. Even though I knew she needed me, I didn't stay and watch out for her. No wonder she died.

Grandma's House

I n New York, we lived in a beautiful home. There was a floor-to-ceiling wall of books in the living room. We had two relatively new cars in good condition. We were a comfortable, middle-class family.

My New York family went to the house where Winnie had grown up every Sunday for midday dinner. Guinevere and Edwin Wasser had built the house in 1920 to welcome their new baby girl Winifred. Edwin had died many years before my time, but Guinevere still lived in the house, and her sister, Beatrice, had moved in once Edwin was gone.

The stone house sat on a tree-lined corner. It faced onto a tree-lined block with a pond at the end of the street. Mr. Simon, of Simon & Schuster, along with daughter Carly, lived across the street. Grandma remarked disdainfully that Carly was "held together with safety pins," disapproving of Carly's outfits not being repaired when there was a rip or a missing button. Not to mention Carly's hippie style.

The house sat on a half-acre of land. There was a fifty-foot terrace along one side, and a large side yard filled with grass and trees and flowers. The yard had a small, one-room playhouse that Rennie and I loved. Inside was child-sized furniture, a table and chairs, and a miniature green-and-white enamel stove, just like the full-sized Glenwood Duplex stove in the main house.

A slate walkway led from the street up to the front door. As I walked along, I passed a fountain with a life-sized cherub in the middle, pouring water from a jug balanced on his shoulder. The water from the jug fell gently into a small, round pond. Grandma's beautiful house was featured in *Architectural Digest* the year it was built.

Grandma's maiden name was Wertheim. She was born and lived her early life in Ames, Iowa. Her father was Solomon Wertheim, and he and his family were the "town Jews." Solly owned the general store in downtown Ames. Guinevere and Beatrice must have been an active pair of young troublemakers because they were known around town as "Solly's Indians."

Perhaps I only imagine that Guinevere was named for Guinevere of the Royal House of Arthur, but it would be apt. Similarly, I think her sister Beatrice was named after Beatrice Portinari who lived in Florence in the twelfth century and was the beloved inspiration of Dante. Her fictional counterpart was the beautiful guide who leads him through Paradiso. I had good step-ancestors.

On Sundays, I enjoyed sitting next to my new great-aunt Beatrice. I admired her crocheting. I still have the eight pale-blue crocheted placemats that she made to perfectly match the eight blue linen napkins with white piping around the edges.

Both Guinevere and Beatrice were college graduates. Higher education was still rare for girls in 1910, but Iowa State University, located in Ames, was co-educational from the start. It was the first public university in the nation to admit women on an equal basis with men. In those days, if a woman did attend college, she was likely to study teaching or library science. Another accepted field for women was home economics, which was Guinevere's college major.

In New York, Guinevere met and married Edwin Wasser. Edwin, like many a New York Jewish boy of the era, had gone to work in the garment industry. He did well. Around 1920, with two partners, he purchased a warehouse on the Charles River in Waltham, Massachusetts, and turned it into a bleachery. Textile mills all over New England sent their fabrics to bleacheries as a final step before the fabric arrived in New York's garment district to be cut and sewn into clothing. Eventually Edwin bought out his partners.

The Waltham property alone became valuable by the time Edwin died, and Guinevere rented it to an upcoming new Massachusetts electronics firm, Litton Industries. What a coincidence that, in eighth grade math class, I had made a such a good investment in Litton Industries, even if it was only an imaginary investment.

Edwin Wasser lived and worked in New York, and he paid close attention to the New York Stock Exchange. Like many well-informed investors, Edwin was smart enough to sell all his stock in the days before the 1929 stock market crash. Edwin and Guinevere did not suffer losses in the crash.

Upon entering Grandma's house, there was a small foyer of golden oak—the floors, the wainscotting, and the furniture gleamed with warm-colored wood. A staircase rose up to the next floor. The living room was large enough to tuck the Steinway concert grand into a corner without any crowding. In another corner was a full bar.

Grandma's Limoges candy dish was always full of chocolates, still in their pleated brown papers. The living room bookcases held all kinds of interesting volumes, including a fake book with no pages that secretly held a silver whiskey flask. The flask was empty, but the book delighted me, and I would take it down from the shelf frequently and open it just to enjoy the existence of such a thing.

Tapestries hung on the walls, Oriental rugs covered the floors, and the living room even had a phone booth. The phone booth door was made of wide, dark wooden planks. An old-timey candlestick telephone silhouette had been cut out of the door. The phone inside the booth was the same candlestick shape, with a rotary dial and a speaking tube on a hanging cord.

Sunday dinner was held in a dining room. We sat around a heavy dark table from Spain. Georgia was the cook, and her husband, Frank, was the driver. They were Europeans but they both spoke English well. Frank drove Grandma everywhere in her blue Chrysler Custom 300. A real leopard-skin blanket was always in the back seat, heavy, soft, and warm against the New York winters.

During dinner, Grandma would summon the next course by pressing a buzzer meant to be within reach of her foot under the table. But it wasn't quite near enough, so the buzzer was always hard for her to reach. Grandma had to slump down in her chair, stretching and extending her leg, trying to locate the small bump under the carpet that would summon Georgia. I often worried that Grandma might slip out of her chair and slide all the way down onto the floor under the table.

Guinevere collected early American pressed glass in a dozen or so different patterns. Her collection was displayed in the breakfast room, in several china cabinets. A few years after my arrival, Grandma asked me which set I wanted to inherit. I picked a pattern called beaded grape. The pieces were a rich green glass, and most were square, which I liked. In 1985, when Grandma died at age eighty-nine, I received more than one hundred pieces.

Moments of Knowing

Guinevere and Edwin invited New York's Jewish society to dine. My sense was that the couple had enjoyed their lives together. Grandma kept a full-sized portrait of Edwin in the dining room. After her death, the American Textile History Museum was interested in having the portrait.

Overweight

I n the black-and-white photos of me as a six-year-old, anyone can see the stripes on my T-shirt curving out a little
around the middle. I wasn't fat. I was just a little bit round
in a cute way. I remember my childhood as full of movement,
running as fast as I could, roller skating up and down sidewalks
for so many hours that my feet would vibrate in bed at night.
All summer long, every day, I spent hours in the Riverdale
Neighborhood House pool, crowded and lively with all the
children from Riverdale. I was proud when I could finally do
an underwater handstand, and I spent months working up the
courage to jump off the high board. I spent so much time in the
water that by the end of the day, my fingers were shriveled up
like little sausages.

At twelve years old, I was five foot seven, and I weighed 127
pounds. No one would have called me fat. But once my mother
died, I could never get enough to eat. I turned to food because
a mother embodies a child's security in this world. With her
death, I had no security left.

◦≈◦

I was in a new school with lots of well-dressed kids who were
much more sophisticated than I was. I had always had the high-

est grades in California and Georgia schools, but my new class-mates were intimidating. They had big homes and beautiful clothes and confidence. Few of them were very nice to me, or even noticed me. I wanted to fit in, but my life had been too different from theirs. Everything was new, intimidating, and iffy.

Looking back, I can see none of this is surprising. I had come face-to-face with death at an early age. And as much as I loved my new life of luxury and safety, having a whole new life might mean yet another new life tomorrow. And who knew if that would be a better life or a worse one.

I soon discovered food was safe. Eating felt good. It took my attention off my circumstances. Food became my best friend, the friend who never asked for anything back.

Winnie had lost some weight, maybe twenty pounds, when she was eighteen. She was proud of this and considered it an important achievement in her life. She lost the weight on the Mayo Clinic Diet. It annoyed me that a thin person considered herself an expert on losing weight after a mere twenty-pound loss.

Still, it was true that all four of us in this new family tended to gain weight. Winnie elected herself to be the "person who had previously solved that problem." She would now show the rest of us how it was done. Since she cooked our meals and chose our foods, we were all put on the Mayo Clinic Diet, without any regard for what we wanted or didn't want to eat.

My mother was from Georgia, and she had been a great southern cook, making biscuits and gravy, fried chicken, and other comfort foods that I loved. But now I found myself on a dietary desert island. Breakfast was a glass of skim milk and one soft-boiled egg. Lunch in a bag for school was a bologna sandwich on white bread, no mayo. I made the bologna sand-wich myself each night and put it into a brown paper bag so that it was ready to go out the door the next morning. Dinner was plain broiled meat or chicken, a side-dish vegetable, either frozen or canned, and another glass of skim milk. I was five feet seven and 127 pounds. I didn't need to eat this spartan diet. I wasn't fat. Yet.

Tension around food filled our house. Food was bad. Food could hurt someone and make them fat. Beware of food! Only eat things that don't taste good and have low calories. These foods were dangerous: pasta, potatoes, bread, sauces, desserts. They could ruin someone's life.

The cookie situation was telling. Winnie kept all the cookies in a double-door cabinet in the kitchen. There were Oreos, Chips Ahoy, Mallomars, Vienna Fingers, Nilla Wafers, and more. The cookie shelf was a dreamland of familiar boxes of sweetness, a reliable oasis of treats. I could pop one in my mouth and forget about the stepmother, the stepsister, the dad who was always at work, the school where I didn't measure up, and the worst meals ever.

The cookie shelf was at about eye level, but I couldn't look inside because Winnie had locked the double cabinet doors shut. Each of the two cabinet doors had a knob, and she had hooked them together with a long-shackle padlock, about four inches long. Once the two doorknobs were joined by the padlock, I couldn't open the cabinet, and I couldn't see the cookie shelf.

Most nights after dinner, I was the only one downstairs, watching the big, black-and-white sixteen-inch TV set in the dining room. Everyone else retired upstairs—Rennie to be alone in her room to read, my parents to have some time together without kids. This was my time to prowl the kitchen.

I would tiptoe from the dining room to the kitchen, open the refrigerator door without a sound, then silently make sandwiches and other delights. If I heard someone coming down the stairs, I hid everything in a hurry and rushed back to the TV, as if I had been there all along. I lived a secret after-dinner life.

Cookies were the main attraction. After the lock appeared, it didn't take me long to learn that I could reach my arm under the padlock and get my hand up onto the shelf, finding my way into an already-opened box of cookies and then bringing out a few to enjoy. I would take a handful, then tiptoe back to sit in front of the TV and enjoy the contraband.

One day I looked in the drawer right below the padlocked cookie doors, and there were the keys to the padlock, easily available, almost as if someone had wanted me to find them. Curious, but welcomed. No more straining my wrist to get to the cookies.

When company was expected, Winnie would make her special company dish, French onion dip, the premiere appetizer of the 1950s. She set it out on the living room coffee table in a fluted crystal bowl surrounded by crackers on a matching crystal plate. I adored this food item. I mastered scooping up just a little as it sat in the fridge awaiting the company's arrival, then smoothing out the top with the spoon so no one would notice. The recipe was sour cream and Lipton's French Onion Soup powder. Divine. I make it to this day and still love it.

Sometimes I even put it into Winnie's crystal bowl on her crystal platter, both of which I inherited. It tastes even better that way. I know this is low-rent '50s' food. But once forbidden, forever desired.

The stricter the rules, the more weight I gained. Soon I wasn't just plump anymore. When I looked in the mirror, all I saw was a fat girl. I was approaching two hundred pounds.

My parents tried to help. In my junior year of high school,

the family doctor gave me a new thing called diet pills. Once I started taking them, I became the "real me." That was how it felt. I was getting thinner and thinner. I was also busy, nervous, my room was spotless, and I got straight A's. I talked endlessly, mostly about myself, and I was late for everything because every situation had so many details to take care of.

Once I was thin, the popular kids befriended me. This was amazing, as I had been ignored by them for the prior four years in school. Suddenly, they invited me to their parties. The girls decided Bob Adelbom from around the corner should be my boyfriend. Being accepted by this group and being invited to their social events made life close to perfect. Bob and I didn't have much in common, but we bowed to the will of the powerful group. We went for walks together and kissed once or twice without much excitement.

I was so delighted to be courted by the popular kids, that I was unable to see things as they were. I was still the exact same person who had been fat and therefore rejected by them. The system that now made me acceptable because I was thin was the exact same system that had judged me fat and unworthy of attention for years. But did I care? Absolutely not. I was going to their parties! What could be better? Who wants ugly fat people around anyway? We thin people were clearly superior.

After a time, the diet pills began to lose their effect. The original dose that had been prescribed was no longer enough to curb my appetite. No worries, the doctor just upped the dose. But then, after a few months, he had to up the dose again. And again. After eight months or so, I was taking so much Dexedrine that the doctor could no longer increase it.

My appetite was back, and I began to eat more. No one knew anything about diet pills in those days. These early diet pills were just speed, Dexedrine primarily. And speed kills your appetite. For a time. Then speed wears off and you have to take more and more to maintain the effect, until you don't dare take any more. And then you gain all the weight back. In the fifties no one had yet experienced the yoyo syndrome of losing weight with diet pills and then gaining all the weight back. And then doing that again. And again.

I was ravenous. I started eating just like before the pills. I gained all the weight back in six months. My parents were furious at me for "cheating." They had "spent a fortune" taking me to doctor's appointments and paying for the pills, and now I was willfully ruining everything. Once again, it was all my fault.

The popular kids dumped me as soon as I gained weight back and so did the boyfriend. My six months of being one of them were over and done. I went back to being the old me, with a few friends on my block. Life went on as before.

I was heartbroken. I would never be accepted by anyone. I was just a fat person.

It would be another twenty years, well into my thirties, before I stopped getting diet pills illegally, or worse yet, snorting meth to prevent my weight from exceeding two hundred pounds. Twenty years of hating my body, of being too heavy to move around easily, of seeking solace in food. I overate every day. I could easily eat a dozen cookies or a couple of sandwiches. I loved bread and starches and sweets.

Finally, when I was in my forties, I found the exact therapy that I needed. I was lucky to find a skilled therapist who specialized in eating disorders. More about that below but suffice for now to say that I truly found peace around food and around fat.

I saw clearly how overweight people were discriminated against in our society. I thought back to the months of being accepted by the "popular" kids in high school. I was still the same person who had been fat a few months earlier, but now

I was suddenly acceptable. I realized how our society valued appearance over a person's inner being and capacity for creativity, understanding, kindness, and caring. I wasn't buying it anymore. I had found a way to accept myself at long last.

In my entire life, I never lost any weight with a diet. I would lose some weight, but I always gained it back again faster than I had lost it. Always. And then some. I stuck faithfully to every diet that had ever been invented, but I always gained the weight back. I went to Weight Watchers and counted points. I went to Nutrisystem and paid them a small fortune. I went on the Atkins diet and peed on little purple sticks to see if I was in ketosis. I became a vegetarian for a whole year. I had eight small meals a day. I fasted and ate absolutely nothing for thirty days. I tried everything there was. Nothing worked, and I was still fat.

When I was about forty years old in the 1980s, weight loss surgery appeared as an option. I was interested. It took me a number of years to find the right way to do this. A friend had a surgery called a duodenal switch. I watched her lose half of her 250 pounds. A year after her surgery, she was a healthy 125 pounds. She came to me and suggested I might want to have the same surgery. She told me she trusted her surgeon, "Dr. K," and gave me all his information.

I had the surgery. The operation removed part of my small intestine, and as a result, less of the food I ate was actually absorbed. The surgery worked.

Today I have a healthy body weight. I am able to go walking and do Pilates, and I feel healthy and fit. I was 350 pounds at my top weight. Without the surgery, the strain on my heart probably would have killed me. I am happy to be alive. And not fat.

For me, one of the best parts of this story happened many years later. The cookie lock situation revealed its true nature. When I was in my thirties, my stepmother Winnie and my dad divorced, and she moved into her own apartment. Rennie had died, and it had been devastating to Winnie. My father married his third wife, and he now lived thousands of miles away. Winnie's parents were both gone, and she had been an only child. I became her only living relative.

I would visit her often. I felt gratitude for all she had done for me over the years, and I wanted to be there for her, to stand by her. She had no one else, and I didn't want her to feel so alone.

Despite all our difficulties Winnie had changed my life. She gave me books to read, taught me about music, and showed me how a person could do artwork as part of their life. She had stood up for me when I was underestimated at the new school. I was grateful to her for how she had opened my life up to creativity and a sense of worth, how she had introduced me to the world of reading, thinking, and exploring the mind.

During these visits with her, I noticed there were no cookies in her apartment. I knew she loved cookies. It took me a while to figure out where they were. Finally, one evening, after dinner, she threw on her coat and found her car keys.

"Where are you going at this hour?" I asked.

"Just to get some cookies," she replied.

"I'll go with you," I replied, my curiosity piqued.

We put on our coats, went down the hall to the lobby, took the elevator to the parking lot, and walked past fifty cars until we came to hers and she opened the trunk.

In the trunk were at least ten different boxes of cookies: Oreos, Mallomars, Chips Ahoy, Ginger Snaps, and good old Nilla Wafers. All my old friends from the padlocked cookie closet of my childhood. This was just a new version of the cookie lock.

Finally, I understood. The cookie lock had never been about me.

Therapy

Therapy was helpful to me throughout my life. When I was sixteen and in high school, things at home in Scarsdale were often tense and unhappy. Winnie sent me to see her therapist, hoping he could help with our situation. I had never been in therapy before. I remember feeling that I was in a safe place. The therapist was a kind and gentle man. I was ready to talk.

While I didn't feel any urgency to talk about the situation at home, I did want to talk about Art and my having been molested. This was remarkable because I had never told anyone about it. I carried my secret with me.

This early experience with therapy was an unexpected opening. It all came pouring out as I told the therapist all I could remember about what happened, and how it had made me feel. I don't remember the words he said, but I remember he was accepting. He didn't judge me. For the first time, I thought maybe I was not at fault. After a few visits, I felt a new lightness and freedom. I no longer had to guard this terrible secret. Therapy had changed my life. For the first time.

My second experience with therapy was in my twenties, I got married to Shelly, my college boyfriend. Our marriage lasted only eleven months. I could not imagine a greater failure. I had always sworn to myself that I would never get a divorce. My parents' divorce had cost me years of suffering—years of crossing the country back and forth between them, years of feeling bad about not wanting to be with my mother, years of being around Art. Getting a divorce was a confirmation of my lack of character. I remembered how therapy had helped me before. I was working and making enough money to try it again. I found a therapist.

Zachary was a psychiatrist. He felt like someone from my own generation, even though he was older than me. He was smart and kind. Seeing him was a comfort and a refuge, a place where I could be completely me. I saw him privately for two years. I worked through my feelings that the divorce was my fault, and it had occurred because I was fat. I began to come to terms with my recklessness and my thirst for danger and adventure. I got a job teaching for Head Start, a very different experience from clerical temp jobs. I found my own new friends and a place to live that I liked. I started looking closely at what mattered to me.

At the end of that time, Zachary joined with Rachel, a nurse psychotherapist, and together they started a therapy group with seven of us. This group met every week in Rachel's basement den. We met for five years. I bonded with every person in the group, and I believe that every person in the group bonded with every other person in the group. No one new ever joined the group, and no one ever left. We were kind to one another. We cared about one another. We worked through life problems for each other. I benefited greatly. I went back to school and discovered I liked achievement as much as adventure . . . that I could live inside the law and be happy.

After four years, the group decided to disband after one more year. We all felt we had reached new levels of understanding about our lives and relationships. We were ready to cherish this experience, and then move on.

Therapy

For that final year, we greatly valued our time together. This was one of the most wonderful and helpful groups I have ever been a part of. I will always be grateful to Zachary, Rachel, and the other members of that group.

~

When I met my husband-to-be Stuart, he told me how much he had been helped by his therapist, Joe O'Connor. This recommendation of O'Connor was one of Stu's many great suggestions, one that changed my life. Stuart recommended O'Connor for many good reasons. O'Connor had helped him to see how difficulties in his early life were still manifesting and holding him back. With O'Connor's help, Stuart's life got better.

O'Connor employed several therapists who practiced his brand of treatment. I worked with a woman named Madeleine. She had an especially calm demeanor that helped me to look at the situations in a slower, more considered way. She worked through my life decisions with me like we were walking a maze, looking at all possible directions, choosing the ones that seemed best.

The O'Connor brand of therapy was more behavioral than my previous experiences. At my first visit, I was surprised to be in the waiting room with half a dozen nuns. OK, nothing wrong with that. O'Connor specialized. I'd never had a conversation with a nun before. Our waiting room conversations were just like conversations with non-nuns, probably more interesting.

I was in the waiting room a long time before every visit. Looking back, I think we were made to wait for our appointments so that we would have an opportunity to socialize in the waiting room with the nuns and other patients. Socializing was not one of my big problems, but I knew it was for many people. For me, it was good to talk with people who were working on themselves.

O'Connor had parties to which all his patients were invited. The parties were held in the waiting room, with music and refreshments. Definitely not the usual approach to therapy. In contrast, my first therapist, when I was sixteen, had a back door so that I could leave his office without walking back through the waiting room and possibly encountering another patient. It seemed like the office was set up to protect patients from knowing about one another. At that time, visiting a therapist might have been seen by some as a very bad sign.

O'Connor's therapy was practical. I had assignments. Madeleine suggested to me that I take flying lessons. This was far from anything I would ever have done on my own. I was afraid, and no doubt that was a part of why she recommended it. Madeleine told me about a small airfield an hour away. I made an appointment for a first lesson. It was exciting. I loved seeing the familiar buildings from above. I remember the piloting instructor saying that the library looked exactly like a great big toilet made of brick.

The piloting experience was a complete picture of my being afraid to do something that would broaden my horizons, then doing it anyway in spite of my fear, and finally seeing how it benefited me. I wasn't interested in taking any more flying lessons, but from then on, this flying lesson experience was a reference.

I would never have gone back to school for my master's degree in computer science without Madeleine and O'Connor. Without their counseling, I would never have gone to such a good school. Before going back to university, I had already become fascinated with computers. I had completed a three-month trade school course and learned programming. I had quickly found a job I liked.

Madeleine and O'Connor saw something more in me—I had a great respect for traditional academics and a degree would be very satisfying for me. They also knew my stepmother had gone to an Ivy League college, and that I barely dared to have such an ambition. They encouraged me. I went back to school and took the prerequisites. Within a year I was admitted to an Ivy League school. I received my masters in computer science. Not only did I learn a great deal, but I have always felt proud of that degree.

~

My fourth experience in therapy still amazes me.

I spent seven years in therapy working on my eating disorder. All my life, I had just believed there was no answer to my distress and unhappiness about being overweight. But after those seven years, I was at peace with my body and weight. It was a remarkable change in my life, one that set free a greater enjoyment of life and a greater flow of creative energy.

I discovered I was a "compulsive overeater." I read *Fat Is a Feminist Issue*, by Susie Orbach. This book changed my life. Susie was Princess Diana's therapist. She was also my therapist's therapist. She understood why women overate. She understood why I was overeating. I spent seven years with this therapist, and when I was done, I had finally found a measure of peace about food and fat.

There were some very simple principles to eating disorder therapy. One was, "Eat when you're hungry and stop when you're full." It sounded so simple, but when I tried to do it, I realized I had no idea what hunger felt like. I had always eaten before I got hungry. I learned to wait and look for the hunger. Stopping when I was full was another journey of discovery. I had to actually pay attention to my body and how it felt. This was new.

Another principle: there is no such thing as good food or bad food. This idea required me to reorganize my entire attitude toward eating. My food world was harshly divided down the middle. Good food was tasteless and without calories. Bad food had sugar and fat and I loved it. I loved it even more for the very fact that it was bad.

My therapist had me keep my favorite bad food, Oreos, in the glove compartment of my car. According to her, not only were the Oreos not bad, but they needed to be readily available. I learned that all food is good food. I needed to listen to what food my body was asking for. I had never listened before.

There was food, and then there was also fat. My therapist guided me as I began to feel that I could be okay with my body, just as it was. I didn't need to lose weight to be okay. This was me. This body had served me well and gotten me through life to this point. I would walk and talk and write and paint. I had friends and adventures and goals and achievements. I arrived at a place of peace with being heavy. It was just the way it was. I could be whomever I wanted to be without losing a pound.

I learned how food and fat are so often sources of anguish for women in our culture. It wasn't just me. What if I were okay just the way I was? I came to a new kind of peace about my body.

Two years with Zachary, five years in group therapy, three years with O'Connor, and finally the seven years I spent in eating disorder therapy. A total of seventeen years.

I am very proud to say that I spent those seventeen years in therapy dredging through my past and considering my future.

Therapy

As embarrassing as it is to have taken so many years, I figured myself out. I relived the trauma of being sexually molested. I understood how compulsive eating related to being abused as a child. I remembered what it was like when my mother was out of control. I revisited the difficulties of moving so often, of always being the new kid in school. I came to terms with my insatiable desire for food and how it anesthetized me. I finally saw myself.

And I finally saw there were things to like in what I saw. I realized I might actually be a smart person, maybe even a funny person. I saw that I loved people, and I loved helping people. Not so bad, I thought. Maybe I could be okay. Just maybe.

I would never have survived without the kind and patient therapists who helped me. I would never have reached the clarity I enjoy today without their giving me the space and the time to talk, to tell it all, to review what I had been through, and to share it with another human being. I am eternally grateful for therapy.

Temple University

I was a C student in high school. Studying wasn't something that even occurred to me. I could shine in English class, have fun in math class, and get through the rest with a grade of C, all without much effort. I didn't think of myself as smart. I had smart family on my dad's side and compared to them, I was average.

In 1961, when I was eighteen, I started college at Temple University in Philadelphia. Temple was easy to get into. It wasn't competitive. No one wanted to go to a big city school in the ghetto in Philadelphia—except me. It was just a two-hour drive from home in Scarsdale, just far enough away, but not so far as to make me nervous or feel alone.

My tuition at the college of liberal arts was $400 a semester, and another $400 for living in the dorm with meals. My four years of college and a bachelor of arts degree cost about $3,200. College costs didn't skyrocket until some years later.

More recently, Temple's tuition alone was about $35,000 a year. The University of Pennsylvania, the Ivy League school across town, was $55,000 a year. Today's prices more accurately reflect the value of education, but I feel sorry for parents and students who have to foot bills like these. I lived in the dorms for all four years of college. I loved the dorm I lived in, Williams Hall. It was a remodeled block of row houses that had been joined together into one residence hall. Williams Hall was warmer and friendlier than the other dorm on campus, a high-rise building.

My first year I was assigned a roommate from New Jersey named Susie Friedman. She arrived with many suitcases of clothes and many pairs of shoes. The first week of school, she went to a mixer and met her new boyfriend, later to be her husband. When she came home that first night, she told me about meeting him and how excited she was.

He had told her that he planned to be President of the United States. As preposterous as this sounds, as time went by, I thought it might happen. That first year, he was elected president of our freshman class, and in our final year, he was elected president of the entire student body. He and Susie got married, and he went on to become president of Temple University Law School. On graduating, he got a job in Harrisburg working for the state governor. I was surprised that was the last I ever heard of him.

I became an English major. Temple's English department had the most interesting professors. The discussions of the many books we read were mostly fascinating. English majors got assigned an enormous amount of reading, but happily, I had always loved reading. I also liked writing, and I did a lot of that as well.

The diary I had kept when I was twelve was a lifeline for me. It was my only forum for telling the whole truth about my life. Through that diary, I realized the power of writing. It was not only a way to communicate my deepest thoughts, hopes, and fears with others, but it was also a way for me to better understand what was happening in my life.

Moments of Knowing

I wrote stories and essays. One day I brought them all to a professor who had offered to review them and give constructive criticism. We made an appointment for a few weeks later for him to return everything and give me feedback. This was in the early 1960s, in the days before there was easy access to copiers. I handed him the only copies of everything I had written, painfully typewritten originals, about fifty pages.

A few weeks later I showed up for our second appointment, looking forward to hearing what he thought of my work. The professor looked sheepish and said, "I am so sorry, but I left my briefcase on the train, and all of your writing was in it."

I was astounded. "What?" I asked. "You lost all my work? Those were my only copies!" I was devastated. I felt a terrible emptiness. I hadn't realized how much I valued my writing, that it was part of my sense of self-worth in this world. And now it was gone. I didn't write again for fifteen years.

I don't remember how any of my college professors looked physically, except him. I can see him now. Kind of a hippie look, chinos, and a suede jacket, casual for an English professor, many of whom wore suits and were more formal. I have forgotten his name, but I will always remember him. His losing my work changed the course of my life. I am just grateful that I found my way back to writing, even though it took me a decade and a half. And I am also grateful to have realized that anyone can leave a briefcase on a train, and it doesn't make them a villain.

I enjoyed most of my liberal arts classes at Temple. I only had to take one political science class and one sociology class, neither of which interested me. I had had six years of French in Scarsdale but still had to take two more years to fulfill the college language requirement. I took a course in medieval French literature. We read *La Chanson de Roland*, written in the year

1100. I didn't relate to it. It was written too long ago, and my French was probably too skimpy to take it all in.

I took Psychology 101 to fulfill my science requirement. Because I took psychology, I never took any courses in the hard sciences, like physics and chemistry. I avoided those classes without even thinking about it, never realizing I had left a big hole in my understanding of things.

By the start of my senior year, I had completed the required courses for graduation. I could take anything I wanted. I picked courses for fun. I took Italian 101. I remember one sentence from that course: "*Limone e fragola sono due sapori che non vane d'accordo.*" Translation: "Lemon and strawberry are two flavors that don't go well together." Imagine how wonderful it was, fifty years later, sitting in a restaurant in Rome, when a waiter brought me a dish of lemon and strawberry ice cream. I had waited so long to say my only Italian phrase.

Another elective that looked interesting to me was physics for liberal arts students. We discussed relativity theory and the nature of the universe and didn't have to memorize many equations. I enjoyed the course very much. I had hoped it might fill the gap I already felt from having no real science studies in my background. But it didn't. It was more of a philosophy course than a science course.

Temple English majors were required to take two entire semesters of, "The Novel in English Literature." I had left this final requirement for the last year, knowing the workload would be demanding. It seemed like we had to read every novel ever written. Emphasis was on early novels, starting with Samuel Richardson's *Pamela*, which we learned was generally considered the first novel. It's about a fifteen-year-old maidservant fending off inappropriate advances from her employer. A timeless plot, as seen in many a contemporary TV series.

Moments of Knowing

The novel course next moved on to Laurence Sterne's, *Tristram Shandy*. This book surprised me as I discovered that authors from the 1700s could be just as creative and wacky as authors today. I could enjoy Sterne and other authors from long ago. We read other important novels by Jane Austen, the Brontë sisters, Thomas Hardy, and Dickens. Reading these books reinforced for me the idea that writers from the past had as much to say to me as contemporary writers.

Reading these books also showed me one of the great benefits of discovering history. I realized that people have always been people. They have always been contemporary, always been smart and creative, and always had fresh ideas. Before this, I thought of history as a lot of people who didn't understand much, and that the important work of the human race was happening now. I didn't even realize I thought this until my preconceptions were challenged by these early novelists. Their work showed me they were every bit as quirky and interesting and just as "alive" as the writers of today.

By the time I graduated, I had read so many books that I never wanted to read another. My first year after college, in 1965, I did not read a single book. Instead, I subscribed to ten different Marvel Comics. I had loved comic books when I was younger. My favorite was Little Lulu. Looking back, I realize now that Lulu was a girl ahead of her time, a headstrong female character. She was decisive and confident. When she was selected as a flower girl, she walked down the aisle strewing banana peels. Lulu was clever and always into mischief. Little Lulu was my first feminist role model. I identified with her.

I also loved Felix the Cat. When they stopped making Felix the Cat comic books, they sent me Tom and Jerry comic books instead. I never liked Tom and Jerry, especially in their failed attempt to replace Felix.

Temple University

In 1965, Marvel Comics had only been around for about five years. Marvel had a new level of creativity and realism not seen before in comic books. I was smitten. I subscribed monthly to ten different comic books. They arrived in the mail on the first of the month, each one folded in half longways and wrapped in a brown paper sleeve.

My lifelong approach, when selecting from several good choices, is to pick my favorite first, just in case I don't live long enough to make it to the next one. This way, I'm always experiencing my current favorite. With comics, *The Silver Surfer* was always the first. Next, I loved *Dr. Strange* because of the spiritual emphasis. *The Fantastic Four* heroes were a good crew. I didn't care much for *The Hulk*, featuring an overly muscular humanoid with green skin. But once all my prior favorites had been read, *The Hulk* became the new favorite.

My boycott of books lasted an entire year. I was perfectly happy subsisting in the Marvel universe. Finally, a book came along that broke through to me. It was Hermann Hesse's, *The Glass Bead Game*, also published under the title *Magister Ludi*. The story took place a few hundred years in the future, in a culture dedicated to the development of the mind. Playing the glass bead game was a primary activity throughout the area. The hero was a young student learning how to play.

The game was never quite described, the suggestion being that it was too complex for a mere lay audience to understand. The young student had to study mathematics, music, and history if he wanted to play well. Players needed to be able to make conceptual connections between topics that seemed unrelated at first. The student aspired to become the Master of the Game or the "Magister Ludi." This book brought me back to the world of reading. I was back for life.

My first job after college was teaching English at a private high school in downtown Philadelphia. The school was in the Tenderloin, a seedy area of town with a bad reputation, but with cheap rents. My boyfriend from Temple, Shelly, taught at the same school, and we lived a block apart. We both came from middle-class suburban homes, and we were fascinated with, if sometimes frightened by, the Tenderloin's squalid conditions, homelessness, crime, and prostitution. We drank deeply our first draught of the underside of life.

But we kept ourselves happy, spending lots of time together, exploring movies, poetry, pot, and acid. We were exhilarated with the simple fact that we were adults on our own. After a year, we planned a wedding.

Tarot Cards

I t was 1964. I was twenty-one years old and a junior in college when I saw my first deck of tarot cards. Their symbolism and fine artwork sparked my imagination. Perhaps they reminded me of the deck of trading cards I had loved so much as a child. All I knew was that I had to have my own tarot deck.

Tarot cards are the historical progenitor of the ordinary playing cards we know today. Just like our ordinary deck of cards, the tarot deck has four suits, and each suit has a royal family. The tarot deck also has an extra twenty-two cards, called the trump cards, or the "major arcana." "Arcana" means secrets or mysteries. Each of these twenty-two trump cards depicts an archetype with specific traits, such as the fool, the magician, or the high priestess.

I wanted to understand the symbols shown on the cards. Doomed people were falling to their deaths from the lightning struck tower. A crescent moon was caught in the folds of the high priestess's serene blue dress. The hanged man was upside down on a cross. What did it all mean?

I loved the symbols, and I loved learning the meaning of each card. Once I had a good sense of each individual card, I looked into the meanings for different combinations of cards. I enjoyed showing the cards to friends and explaining their meanings.

Moments of Knowing

Underlying my instantaneous passion for the tarot cards was my schoolyard vow from the kindergarten playground, from the moment of knowing when I vowed I would live for love. If love was to be the primary force in my life, didn't I need to look more deeply into how love worked? And if love was a primary force in the universe, then didn't I need to look more deeply into how the universe worked? Could the tarot cards be a guide to how things worked? I thought maybe. With the tarot cards, I began a more intentional spiritual life. From what I knew of love, it was magic. And not just romantic love. All kinds of love made for great changes in my inner life and relationships.

The first thing I had to do was to buy a deck of tarot cards. I went to my local bookstore, assuming they would carry them. The deck designed by Arthur Waite was the most popular, and still is today. I asked the clerk at the store if he sold them, and he told me tarot cards were illegal in Pennsylvania, where I lived. I was stunned. Illegal? In the twentieth century?

Tarot cards are still illegal in Pennsylvania today. Pennsylvania state law declares that fortune-telling is a crime, so fortune-telling materials like tarot cards are banned as well.

This law was passed because it was supported by two disparate groups usually opposed to one another. The first group was made up of those who supported science against superstition. They believed the spirit world was a hoax and did not exist. Ipso facto, fortune-telling and everything associated with it should be banned.

The second group was made up of devoutly religious Christians, who believed that fortune-telling should be forbidden because it required delving into the Satanic spirit world instead of the godly spirit world. These two groups, with no views in common, combined to form a majority and the law was passed.

Tarot Cards

If found guilty of fortune-telling with tarot cards, I could go to jail for a year. Shades of the Salem witch trials . . .

I scoured other Philadelphia bookstores until I heard about a bookstore on the University of Pennsylvania campus that sold tarot cards. The next morning, there I was, waiting outside when they opened. The store was in a dilapidated row of shops, tucked between a restaurant and a pharmacy. It looked like the kind of offbeat place that might carry something illegal.

I went to the counter with my request, fully expecting a rebuff. But this time was different. The clerk glanced covertly to the left and then to the right. He bent over close so I could hear him as he spoke softly.

"Yes, we do have tarot cards. But you realize it is important to put them into your bag immediately and not let anyone see them?"

I nodded, and he nodded back. He turned around and unlocked a wooden cabinet. He brought out an extra-large deck of cards in a paper box.

Finally. They were in my hand. The front of the box showed the Fool, unknowingly walking toward the brink of a precipice. That seemed a wonderful image to me.

Isn't being a fool the start of every great adventure?

People said that about the tarot. Someone had to be a certain kind of fool to be interested in them, hence the fool on the cover of the box. I was that fool.

I paid for the cards and went out the door, resisting the impulse to open them up on the sidewalk. I forced myself to walk a short way into the leafy Penn campus. Finding a bench under a tree, I sat down, fully engaged in the experience of the moment. I opened the box and spread the cards out into a fan. I took in this new means of accessing another level of reality. I was not disappointed.

Moments of Knowing

I turned the cards over one by one, spending a little time with each. There were so many details on each card. What kind of flowers were those? Why was the sun a baby on a horse? Was that a hawk on the glove of the nine of disks? Every object had meaning—every color, all the relationships between the colors and objects and backgrounds, and even the expressions on the faces. I didn't realize hours went by, not until the hard wooden bench became uncomfortable.

I set out to teach myself more. I found some pamphlets that discussed the meanings of each card. I spent hours noticing subtle details. Why did the angel on the temperance card have one foot on land and the other foot in the water? Water mixed with wine? A kind of balance.

Why did death carry a black flag with a white flower? Apparently, this was a symbol of the natural cycles of life, with the flower in white for purity. Who were the four small figures in the corners of the wheel of fortune card: man, eagle, lion and bull? I learned they had a name, the "tetramorph," which translated to "the four shapes." They represented any set of four elements, but in particular they were associated with Matthew, Mark, Luke, and John. Matthew was the winged man because his writings focused on the humanity of Christ. The lion of St. Mark referred to the majesty of Christ, like the majesty of the king of the beasts. Luke was the bull, traditionally a sacrificial animal, because his writings emphasized the sacrifice of Christ on the cross. And finally, John was the eagle, a symbol of "that which comes from above." Once I knew these things, I saw them elsewhere, such as the lion atop a tall column in Venice's St. Mark's Square.

As I studied the tarot, I never felt like I was working. I enjoyed my efforts to understand the meaning of each card. In time, I learned every card and what it meant. I learned how the symbols on each card create a message.

Tarot Cards

Sometimes I shared the cards with friends. Whenever I had conversations about the cards, threads of meaning always seemed to emerge, threads with meaning for me and for the other person as well. Most of the time we both found the cards helpful. The specific cards we turned over seemed to reflect situations in our lives. And they seemed to suggest helpful approaches to those situations.

As I sit here and write today, my tarot deck is on the table beside me, in its torn box, dog-eared, with masking tape wrapped around to hold it together. The cards have come a long way with me . . . fifty years. Longtime friends.

In subsequent years, as I learned more about spiritual practices, I learned about "be here now," the practice of being present, of maintaining awareness and mindfulness. Ultimately, I set aside the tarot cards with their complex symbolism and overtones of power.

Today, my spiritual work is simplified. I am happy if I can be present to the moment and act with simple kindness. But I am grateful for the rich steppingstone the tarot provided, and I will always feel a deep fondness for them.

D-I-V-O-R-C-E

When I married Shelly right out of college in 1965, we spent lots of time together and were sympatico. He was handsome and taller than me and smart and funny. We both loved books and movies. He liked smoking pot more than I did, but I didn't mind. He was Jewish, and I found that comfortable. Within eleven months we were divorced.

I had stolen him from my dear friend and roommate, Viveka. She and Shelly had been in a relationship for months. Thanks to me, that relationship of hers suddenly disappeared. She was understandably angry at my betrayal, and she cut off our friendship. I was troubled by it but not enough to stop seeing Shelly.

Since high school, I always had to have a boyfriend. It was like there was an empty picture frame entitled, "Boyfriend," and it didn't really matter to me whose picture was in the frame, as long as it was occupied by someone reasonably acceptable. That picture frame could not be empty. I would scout out a new boyfriend and have him lined up and ready as soon as the first signs appeared that Mr. Current Boyfriend might be moving on.

I was driven by this. I could not imagine a world without a boyfriend. The feminist movement was still in the future, and I had no idea that my sense of self-worth depended on there being a man in my life. It was just the way things were. It was normal.

I had lots of girlfriends, and we had lots of conversations. Many of my 1965 girlfriends had similar requirements.

Even today, long after the rise of feminism and the deepening understanding of women's dependency, I still see this same driving need in many women, especially young women who have not yet had the time to learn they will be fine on their own.

I often think of a scene in the 2013 movie, *What the Bleep Do We Know*. Everyone is slow dancing with a partner, and each person is attached to an IV pole on wheels so it can dance along with them. So, there are two people dancing, and the two poles move with them like a foursome. The IVs are metaphorically administering hormones, the chemicals that drive much of our sexual behavior. In response to these inner drugs, most of us will seek a mate.

This search ruled my life for years. For me, hormone-driven behavior kicked in when puberty started and didn't end until my forties. I like to think that my growth and self-knowledge caused this desperate search to end in my forties, but on the other hand, maybe it just ended because the possibility of childbearing ended.

Today, I look back and see that for all those years, an important part of my role on earth was as a pawn in Evolution's game. Most of what I put energy into was finding sex and a relationship with a man. I had no idea that I was driven. It seemed completely normal to me to always be prowling around looking for a boyfriend. Nothing unusual—that's the way it was for everyone. It never occurred to me that evolution was running my life. Running it without my best interests at heart.

Evolution's plan for us doesn't have anything to do with our individual happiness. Evolution just wants us to find a mate and procreate. If we die five minutes later, evolution won't care. She has succeeded as soon as there is a child. And Evolution runs her program in our bloodstream. We are in her grips. She doesn't bother to give us the list of side effects, which would be such a long list she would have to talk faster than one of those drug ads on television. I am horrified to consider how many of my decisions were made by Evolution and her hormone warriors. These decisions had nothing to do with the life that I might have wanted for myself.

Many years after Shelly and I parted ways, I missed Viveka's friendship, much more than I missed him. It was twenty years before she and I found one another again. I told her how deeply I regretted my betrayal of her, and how much I wished to make amends. She understood and forgave me.

Thank you, roommate.

Today I know that when you steal a boyfriend from somebody, the boyfriend you get is stealable. It was only eleven months before someone else stole Shelly from me. The first clue was that he began to look like his old girlfriend. She was the daughter of a family that made pickles in Philadelphia. The pickle brand was Kaplan's, and her name was Carol Kaplan. Shelly had new gold-rimmed glasses like Carol had always worn. And there was something in the way he moved. You know how couples start to look alike? Shelly was not looking like me.

When he broke up with me, he told me I was too fat. I was fat, but I weighed exactly the same as I had when I met him. I weighed exactly what I had weighed for the entire time he had known me, even on the day we got married. It was a lame excuse. But that didn't stop me from torturing myself with it.

He said he would move out in a week or two.

I got up before dawn the next morning. I packed my sandals and my tarot cards and left. As I walked down the street away from our home, I turned around to take one last look. I felt sad as I looked at the door of our meant-to-be-happy home. The first-floor windows were hung with bright yellow linen curtains that I had made by hand, stitching carefully with matching yellow thread, loving our new home, loving our new marriage. And now it was over.

Once I left, I was even more miserable. I moved in with some friends a few blocks away. I felt lost. I floundered around for something to hold onto. I needed a plan. *Hey, how about a new boyfriend? Absolutely! That's a plan that always works for me!*

I needed a book about how to find a boyfriend. Books always had the answers. I went to a bookstore and found, *The Intelligent Woman's Guide to Manhunting*, by Albert Ellis. Ellis was an acolyte of Ayn Rand, my guide when I was twelve years old. Somehow, I managed to put aside all I had learned in the intervening ten years. Once again, I was taking advice from Ayn Rand and company. It's hard to understand, but my need to "manhunt" greatly outweighed any intelligent thinking.

I carefully followed Ellis's instructions. Early one evening, I made my way to a nice park in a nice neighborhood. I found an empty bench and sat down on one end, as per Ellis's directions. I left plenty of space at the other end of the bench for someone to join me. The park was called Rittenhouse Square, and it was surrounded by expensive apartments and exclusive shops in an upscale area of downtown Philadelphia. Only the nicest people came out for a stroll, many with their purebred dogs.

Within minutes of my sitting down on the bench, a man about my own age sat down at the other end and struck up a conversation. The book had worked! He told me his name was Ronnie Richmond. Ronnie was smart and not exactly handsome. A lot of his hair was gone, so he had a big forehead, but that made him look smart. Which he was. Ronnie turned out to be a gifted concert pianist.

He invited me to visit his apartment. I put him off until we had met a few more times in the park. It seemed important to eliminate the serial killer option, even though the book didn't mention it. Finally, I accepted the invite. His apartment was one big room with a Steinway Concert Grand piano filling the space. His mattress was on top of the piano.

I loved listening to Ronnie play. He was brilliant, at least as far as I could tell. I played piano, badly, but enough to understand how skillful he was. For some reason, he wasn't on a world tour being famous and making tons of money. I never discovered why not. Instead, I just enjoyed the best in-the-same-room piano I had ever heard.

After a few visits, I became comfortable in Ronnie's apartment. I would lie on the floor under the piano while he played. This was an exciting way to listen to music. Sound waves vibrated my whole body. I had never heard Chopin in quite the same way.

Life was better now that I was meeting new people like Ronnie. He soon took me to meet his mentor, Larry Konigsberg. Larry was much older than me, probably about fifty, which seemed ancient. He was a good-looking man, powerful, short, and fit. Not that tall, but wide and strong. He always looked full of energy for whatever was happening in the moment. He had blond-going-on-gray hair, and blue eyes he would fix on you in a good way.

He owned a big row house in downtown Philadelphia where he lived with his wife and their four teenage kids. He rented about eight rooms of the house to a number of twenty-something artists. These included painters, writers, dancers, and musicians. Everyone called Larry, "The Big Eagle." He was locally famous.

Ronnie explained to me that The Big Eagle mentored these young people, both in their personal lives and in their artistic professions. He knew downtown Philadelphia gallery owners, theater people, and musicians. He knew his way around the arts community. He had helped many talented people get their start.

It took only a few weeks for me to move into The Big Eagle's group house. I got to know the painters and musicians and writers. The Big Eagle's wife, Sylvia, was a painter as well . . . a fine painter who sold lots of her work.

We had group dinners every night. The Big Eagle's house was more than a place to live. It was a way of life, wrapped up in the house, wrapped up in Larry's world view. But it was a pretty good world view. Take responsibility for yourself, work hard, explore your creativity, clean house in your mind, and things will work out.

Sylvia cooked for everyone and was a very perceptive and intelligent woman. I loved helping her in the kitchen, cutting up onions, peppers, and mushrooms for a giant stir-fry to feed ten or twenty. I could talk to Sylvia about cooking, painting, or life. I looked up to her as a well-known artist, respected throughout the city, and I looked up to her as a wise woman.

Larry had a few friends his own age, and they frequently came to dinner. They were like Larry, open-minded, individualistic, and smart. Sometimes Larry and his older friends had meetings around the dining room table in the evening. They called themselves the Suicide Club. There was no suicide involved, but the heaviness of the group name underlined how seriously they took these meetings.

They would invite one of the younger male artists/musicians/poets to join them. These older guys would grill the younger one about his purpose in life, what he was doing, what it meant to him. The young artist would be forced to say out loud what his life was about and why it mattered. We all respected the Suicide Club. It didn't seem to hurt anyone, and it seemed to make things clearer for the younger ones who went through the process.

Of course, every single person at the Suicide Club table was male, both the older ones and their younger subjects. It was 1966, and that seemed perfectly normal. Looking back, I can see we thought it was only men who needed to navigate their lives with awareness and consciousness. Women just had to find and follow one of those good men.

The Big Eagle advised everyone on everything. He often spoke in a booming voice to underline his opinions. Luckily for me, his advice was good, and he helped me to move beyond my broken marriage and into a new life of my own.

I was given a small room on the second floor. It had a window overlooking an alley, and a tall Ailanthus tree (also known as a slum tree) grew out of a grate in the alley. I was pleasantly surprised later on, to learn that my beautiful slum tree was also known as a "tree of heaven." The tree filled my window with delicate greenery. Larry built me a bed from two-by-fours and plywood. I felt welcomed and like I finally had a new home.

There was a grand piano that filled the front room of the house. Ronnie Rich would frequently play, and everyone would listen and enjoy. When Ronnie wasn't around, I sometimes played. One time I took off the ruby engagement ring Shelly had given me, which I had yet to return to him. I always took off my rings to play piano.

The ring had belonged to his mother, someone I cared for and whom I missed now that I was no longer married to her son. When I finished playing, I left the piano room without remembering to put my ring back on. About an hour or two later I came back, but the ring was gone. I never saw it again.

The ring's disappearance cast a shadow over the community. Someone was a thief, but I never found out who it was.

Winnie had taught me the societal rules about engagement rings. If the man broke off the marriage, then the woman didn't have to give the ring back. However, for the sake of his mother, I had intended to return it to him, whenever I saw him again. After we had been separated for a while, Shelly asked me to return it, and I had to tell him how it had been stolen. I was shocked when he accused me of lying so I could keep the ring. That was the real moment of divorce for me. After that conversation, I didn't hear of him or speak to him for forty years.

Then, with the advent of computers, about the time we were both sixty years old, he friended me on Facebook. He said he was divorced again, and his children were mad at him. I felt very sad for him, having to go through it a second time in life. I still feel the pain of the end of our marriage, so devastating for me that it took me years to recover. Despite the difficulties of our parting, I take comfort in my memories of Shelly as a wonderful friend and lover for many years. I truly wish him the best in his life, his heart, and his mind.

Kelly Girl at
the Funeral Parlor

I n 1965, when I first graduated from college, I dreaded going
to some boring job every day. All my work experience had
been clerical, and all my jobs had been mundane . . . mundane typing and mundane filing.

It was the 1960s, and I identified strongly with the hippie
counterculture. Going to a boring office was not a part of the
adventurous life I had planned. It would be another ten years
before I realized a job could be fun and challenging, something
I cared about. And, I had never even considered that achievement might serve me better than adventure.

I started working for Kelly Girl, an agency that sent temporary workers out to offices for a few days at a time to help with
typing and bookkeeping. I liked being a temp worker because I
didn't have to make a long-term commitment.

I began as a typist, but I soon discovered bookkeeping paid
$4.00 an hour more, a significant amount more when wages
hover around $10.00 an hour. I told Kelly Girl I could do book-
keeping. Not that I knew the first thing about bookkeeping, but
I figured it couldn't be too hard. I had rarely overdrawn my own
account, so what more did I need to know? It turned out I was
fine. Most of what I had to do was add up columns of numbers.

Kelly Girl at the Funeral Parlor

Somehow, working with dollars, expenses, and receipts was not quite as boring as typing, especially with the extra $4.00 an hour.

Kelly Girl sent me to various Philadelphia businesses. I spent a week in the offices of the Phillies baseball team. The office was in the city's Veterans Stadium. Getting there was a long bus ride to the edge of town, but the offices where I worked overlooked home plate from windows about four stories above the playing field.

It was fun being at the stadium. On my arrival, I rode up in an elevator lined in bright-green AstroTurf—the floor, the walls, and even the elevator ceiling. All the carpets throughout the stadium offices were AstroTurf. I wondered if these people had it in their living rooms at home.

I sat at my desk doing my bookkeeping while baseball executives came and went. These important men observed an interesting dress code. They each wore a nice quality, two-button blazer in navy-blue. The buttons on the blazer were large and gold and had the Phillies Liberty Bell insignia. There were smaller gold buttons on the cuffs. Khaki pants were required. The finishing touch was a pair of brown-and-white saddle shoes. It was a middle-aged version of eternal youth.

In contrast, the majority of my own wardrobe was made up of three pairs of denim jeans and four tie-dyed shirts. Each day, I struggled to piece together a suitable business outfit. My one black A-line skirt got a lot of wear, and a hand-crocheted black hippie shawl was almost as good as a jacket. Also, it mostly covered up the tie-dyed shirts.

Kelly Girl sent me to different kinds of businesses: insurance offices, offices of a family-owned chain of drug stores, and a movie theater. I liked getting a look at the back end of various enterprises. The most unusual place Kelly Girl sent me to was a funeral home.

Moments of Knowing

I was in my early twenties. Mortality was not something I thought about. Like most twenty-somethings, I took it for granted that my life would go on forever. Of course, I knew about death—my mother had died, after all—but at some level I assumed it didn't apply to me. Going to a funeral home was interesting to me. It was a world I knew nothing about. I drank in the details.

Now, when I look back, I can see that my short time at the funeral home changed my sense of what life was all about.

The funeral business was named Elliot M. Dean. It was clear from the first encounter that this was Philadelphia's finest, and they wanted you to know it. The business was located downtown in an historic, five-story row house on a fashionable side street. Downtown Philadelphia had a number of residential streets too narrow for a car, built before the automotive age. The streets were tree-lined and paved with cobblestones. They were quite exclusive places to live and work, these mostly old brick buildings built when America was young.

Elliot M. Dean was in a single marble building in the middle of a long block of brick structures. The marble was significantly more elegant than the surrounding brick. I entered between two marble columns through a heavy wooden door. Once inside, I was at the end of a long, empty hallway that filled most of the first floor. Far at the other end sat a single desk with a receptionist. There was a black telephone on her desk, and nothing else. Her hair was dyed a bit too dark.

"May I help you?" Her voice echoed across the empty hall.

"I'm from Kelly Girl, to help with the bookkeeping," I replied, walking toward her.

"They're expecting you. Please go up to the third floor." She gave me a professional smile and pointed to an elevator door. I pushed the up button, and the elevator door soon opened.

Kelly Girl at the Funeral Parlor

It was a small elevator, with a golden metal grate across the front. There was an actual elevator operator, a confirmation that no expense was being spared. The elevator operator smiled at me as she pulled back the grate. She wasn't tall, and she was a little on the heavy side, but not too much. She wore a navy-blue suit with a light-blue blouse, dressed for the successful place where she worked.

I felt she and I were about to go on a wild adventure together. Her eyes danced, and her big smile was outlined by bright-red lipstick. She had a lot of blond hair growing in many directions. Her hair looked like a sheepskin—fuzzy, curly, and soft. I smiled at her, hoping to make it clear I was open to those fun possibilities lighting up her face.

"You must be the temp. I'll take you up to your floor. And welcome to Elliot M. Dean! When lunchtime rolls around, I would love to give you a tour of the building, if you would like that?" She kept her one hand on the grate and turned her body to face me so we could chat.

"Yes, I'd like that very much!" I smiled at her.

"You look like someone who would be curious about things," she said with another big smile. "And this is quite a place, as you will see. I have worked here for over ten years. And I don't mind working in a funeral home one bit. I find it quite interesting. My name is Morrigan."

I replied, "Morrigan, so great to meet you. I am happy to hear that this is going to be an interesting place for me to work. I look forward to seeing you at lunchtime."

The elevator stopped smoothly at my floor, and Morrigan let me out.

"See you later," she added, as she pulled the grate closed.

In the area where I would work, there were six women, each sitting behind a big wooden desk. The desks were arranged in a large circle, maybe twenty-five feet wide, with everyone facing in. Most of the girls were about my own age, but there was one older woman. She stood up and walked to the single empty desk, beckoning me over. I had no doubt this was the boss.

"Hello, Mary. Welcome to Elliot M. Dean. We are delighted that you will be taking Julie's place for a few days," she said, gesturing toward Julie's empty desk, then pulling the chair out for me. As I sat down, she continued, "This is the main funeral home office. We do all the management and bookkeeping here." With that, she introduced me briefly to the other girls and efficiently showed me how to do my work.

I got right into it. It was always easy for me to lose myself in numbers, making sure everything was legible, that all the columns added up, and that generally, all was accounted for. Before I knew it, it was lunchtime. Everyone headed to the stairs to go out for lunch.

I walked over to the elevator, hoping to collect on my promised tour. Soon Morrigan was pulling back the grate and again welcoming me into her small space.

"Now you already saw the first floor, which is just a reception area. But quite grand, wouldn't you agree?" I nodded enthusiastically. She stopped at the second floor and opened the door but not the grate. "Now this floor has the chapels for the funerals, and the meeting rooms where the families do business with us. There are important gatherings and meetings happening on this floor all the time. We won't get out here so as not to disturb anyone." After our short glimpse, she closed the door, and we went up.

"As you know, the third floor where you work is for management and bookkeeping, so let's go on up to the fourth." Once we stopped, Morrigan opened the door and slid back the grate. She flipped a switch to put the elevator into stop mode.

Kelly Girl at the Funeral Parlor

We both got out, and she led me into a room full of coffins.

"This is where you pick out your casket." A dozen or more caskets were spread around the room, like a car showroom, with the coffins parked facing different ways. The casket lids were opened to display luxurious silk and satin linings and matching small pillows.

"Have you ever seen a casket?" she asked.

"Not really," I replied, somehow a better answer than just "no." She pointed out the discreetly displayed prices, starting at about five thousand dollars, with many going up into the tens of thousands. I could read her raised eyebrows, but she was too loyal to her employer to say anything critical about the prices. Until that day, I had no idea that death was so expensive.

Morrigan walked over to a long rack where various types of clothing hung. There were about ten beautiful nightgowns in different colors and styles. They looked expensive and modest with plenty of cover-up. After the nightgown section of the clothing rack, there was a selection of about ten formal tuxedos for the men.

There was one strange thing about the clothing: nothing was full length. Each garment came down only to just below the waist.

Morrigan explained, "When the person is lying in the casket, they're covered by a satin sheet from the waist down, so the clothes don't need to be full length." I imagined how embarrassing it might be to show up at the Pearly Gates with a bare bottom, but I didn't share that thought.

We headed back to the elevator and rode up the fifth and final floor. A bell indicated someone was summoning the elevator, so when we got to five, Morrigan told me to wander around, and she would be back to get me soon. This was the embalming floor.

Moments of Knowing

As I stepped off the elevator, I saw a man lying on a table about waist high. He was an older man, but handsome with carefully groomed gray hair. He was lying in state, wearing a formal navy-blue military uniform with gold buttons and gold braid trim. His matching navy-blue cap was embroidered with gold leaves on the brim and sported a gilded emblem at the front. The hat was tucked under his right arm. His eyes were closed. Despite his stillness, he looked important.

At that moment, I realized this was the first dead person I had ever seen. I felt curious but a little frightened. Into my mind came the unwelcome thought that I should touch him and see if his skin felt the same as a regular person. I reached out with my index finger and gave the back of his hand a small nudge. He felt kind of stiff. I worried that I had overstepped my bounds, even if he would never know.

From that day to today, I have felt a connection with this man. I had a moment of intimacy with him, even if he didn't know it. Later, I found out his name was Bram Wanamaker, from the famous Wanamaker family, the founders and owners of Philadelphia's premier Wanamaker's Department Store. *Dear Bram, I hope I didn't disturb your sleep on that day.*

I turned away from my quiet new friend to see what else was on the fifth floor. At the other end of the room were two women, each lying on a person-sized marble table. The tables were built over a white tile tub set in the floor, with drainage holes. As I walked over to investigate, I inhaled a sharp medicinal smell. The tables were tilted lengthwise, and each woman was stretched out on her table, heads at the lower end as if their bodies were draining.

Both women were naked, completely uncovered. Both had their hair going in all directions. Each of them had a terrible expression on her face—eyes open, mouth open, head tilted back. I felt like I was invading a final privacy to which these women were entitled. Unlike Mr. Wanamaker, these women no longer looked human. Or had not yet been made to again look human. I did not care to imagine my own body in a room like this.

I barely had time to take this all in when I heard a high-pitched voice behind me. I turned around fast like I had been caught. There was a heavy man standing in the doorway wearing an apron over his suit. He was much older than me. He opened the conversation with, "I see you are interested in science." *Was he referring to the science of dead bodies?*

"I'm interested in science, too," he continued, with barely a pause. "Perhaps you can help me with my scientific experiment. My name is Malcolm, and I'm the chief embalmer for Elliot M. Dean. I am one hundred percent in charge of this area," he said, sweeping his arm across the entire fifth floor. "I dress each body to reflect the person's achievements in life. I prepare all the bodies in the most expert way possible so that they may endure permanently."

He barely paused for breath.

"Now, may I tell you about my other important research?"

I was a bit stunned by his appearance and grandiose opening, not to mention the bizarre setting, but I managed to nod my head.

"I will need to come to your house. I will ask you fifty-six simple questions, but don't worry! I will give you all the answers in advance. Don't be nervous about getting the answers right! You don't have to know anything special to participate in my research. But I'll tell you now that you will have to sit in a chair during the experiment, and I will have to tie you to the chair so that you cannot get up or move around. Any movement whatsoever will interfere with the experimental results. So, can I count on you, considering your obvious interest in furthering scientific understanding?"

I muttered something about needing to think about it. I felt great relief as the elevator arrived. I stumbled toward the elevator and away from the man, feeling a little unstable, like I was hurrying to leave a strange world behind. "Morrigan, I am so happy to see you!" Wasn't that the truth!

"I bet you are," she replied, looking over at the man as she closed the grate and started us safely on our way. "Don't let Malcolm bother you. Everyone round here is just a little crazy." We arrived at the third floor.

"You were so kind to show me around. Thank you!" I said, reaching out to gently touch her shoulder. She gave me one last grin and was on her way.

I walked over to my desk. The other girls were back at work, but a couple of them glanced up to see me returning. I must have looked spooked.

One of the girls observed, "You're white as a sheet. Oh, I bet you met Malcolm!" Now they all looked up, and a few started to giggle. "Don't let him bother you. He has asked every one of us to be in his experiment. He's just a little old and out of touch, that's all."

I nodded at them all to show my gratitude. I was relieved to know I was not Malcolm's only target. "Thanks for sharing that," I replied. "I was a caught off guard." A number of nodding heads and sympathetic smiles warmed me back up.

The workday finally ended. As I left Elliot M. Dean and stepped out onto the street, I breathed in the fresh air of the early evening, grateful to reach the end of the day at the funeral parlor.

The next morning, I called Kelly Girl to explain I was not feeling well and wouldn't be going back to Elliot M. Dean.

Kelly Girl at the Funeral Parlor

Spending the day in a house of death was not the kind of adventure I was looking for. I didn't want to go back.

This experience changed my attitude toward the business of death. For the first time, I realized that some funeral homes may be selling overpriced goods and services to mourning people, people in pain, and people who would spend more than they could afford to honor the ones they loved. I could see where a funeral home might be a dangerous place to go when you were grieving for a lost loved one and money was no object. I'm sure this is not true for all such establishments. But my day at the funeral parlor underlined for me that there could be a great contrast between what was kind and humane, and what people were willing to do to make a living.

Kerry
and Boats

In 1972, I was twenty-eight years old. I had been living at the Big Eagle's house for several months. One day, I met an interesting man coming out of the room next to mine. He had flashing brown eyes and lots of dark hair that hung attractively over his eyes. He had a prominent mustache that I liked. He was only a little bit shorter than me. He was tan, and he looked like he lived an active outdoor life. Not that anybody knew back then that being active and outdoors was healthy and good for you.

"Hi," he said. He stopped and leaned against the wall as if he wanted to spend a little time with me. "I'm Kerry. I think we are next-door neighbors. Looks like my room is right next to yours."

"I haven't seen you before," I said. I leaned against the wall next to him. "Did you just move in?"

"No, I've lived here for years, but I'm in the merchant marine, so I'm gone for months at a time traveling on ships. You must have moved in while I was gone?"

"Yes, I've been here a few months now. How nice to discover I have a neighbor." I liked him, and I could feel he liked me as well. In the next few weeks, we got to know one another, spending time together at the house, going out to eat, and taking walks.

Kerry loved the sea. As a merchant marine, he had traveled the world. He owned his own small boat, an old fishing boat named the *Laura H.* He kept his boat about an hour away on the Delaware Bay, south of Philadelphia, in the small town of Fortescue, New Jersey.

Soon he took me to see the *Laura H.* She was a clunky wooden fishing boat, about forty feet in length and very wide. There was a long, open deck with chairs mounted for five or six fishermen. This was a "party boat," meaning a party of fishermen could rent it for the day. Kerry would take them out to fish on the bay. He provided bait, beer, and sandwiches. He kept trying different likely places on the bay, until he found the place where the fish were biting. Kerry made enough income as a fishing boat captain to cover his boat and all Fortescue expenses. And then some.

I loved being on the boat, and soon he invited me to come along and help out on trips with the paying customers. Kerry was a great teacher. He knew boats, and he taught me everything he could think of. The first thing I learned was which side was port and which side was starboard. We went on from there.

I learned how to tie the boat up to the dock at the end of the day so it would move up and down with the tides and not hang up on the dock lines or be overwhelmed by high tides and possibly sink. Next, I learned how to back the boat out of the slip and sail out into the bay.

Our bait was squid, and soon I was cutting bait like an expert. After I pulled out and threw away the squid's tentacles and guts, I was left with a clean white tube that used to be the squid's body. This tube was about three inches long and half an inch in diameter. If I slit the tube and laid it flat, it was about an eighth of an inch thick. I got good at cutting this into bait—triangular pieces about two inches long, half an inch wide at the top, then tapering to a point. If I put the hook through the wide end at the top, the rest of the bait would wiggle around in the water and attract fish.

I cut bait and served beer and generally worked to keep the customers happy. Kerry didn't ship out in the merchant marine as frequently as he had before, enjoying the warm weather in Fortescue now that he had my company.

After we had been together for some months, we rented a house in Fortescue. It was on the beach of Delaware Bay, a short block from the boat. The house was on the sand, and the entire house leaned into the water. The first floor was just sand and water, so we climbed an outdoor staircase to the second floor. We had windows looking out over the bay, and breezes were always blowing through the slanted house. It was a happy time.

Kerry had a beautiful sense of color and design. I loved that about him. It was because of Kerry that I came to a wonderful realization.

When I am drawn powerfully to someone, it's because I need to learn something that they already know. For me, a big part of attraction is the discovery of a person who embodies qualities and understandings I strongly want to embody myself.

Maybe this is what "falling in love" really is. We admire this person. We treat them well to honor the important things they already know that we want to learn. New understandings travel along the rays of love from their heart to our own. We change in the way we want to change. Love is the fastest teacher of them all.

Pretty soon I picked out colors, hung pictures on the walls, and cooked plates of fish and corn on the cob, serving them alongside sliced Jersey tomatoes.

Kerry and Boats

In my experience, there is no tomato like a Jersey tomato.

Delaware Bay offered us a number of different types of fish. There were blue fish, big, firm, and only a little bit oily. We caught more weakfish than any other fish. Weakfish is another name for a sea bass, white and good to eat. Everyone called them weakies. One of my favorite fish was the porgy, a fat little fish with a buttery taste. Once in a while we would catch a flounder, which in Delaware Bay was called a fluke. Fluke were rare to catch, and the most delicious fish of all.

Kerry had an interest in all things spiritual. This was another strong reason I was drawn to him. One time he was shipping out of Newport News, Virginia, and I drove him down to his ship. Kerry first told me about Edgar Cayce, an American clairvoyant who lived in the early 1900s. Cayce had lived and worked near where we were going. Cayce's history and the information about his work was maintained at the Edgar Cayce Institute in Virginia Beach, not far from Newport News. Kerry suggested I visit the Institute, so after I dropped him off at his ship, I drove there.

Edgar Cayce spoke from a trancelike state. During the first half of the 1900s, people from all over the country would send Cayce questions about healing, reincarnation, and past lives. People who were sick would describe their symptoms to Cayce, and from his trance, he would suggest remedies that were often successful. His reputation spread, and many people turned to him for help. Cayce was a devout Christian, although hardly accepted by more traditional Christians. They denounced him.

There was an extensive card catalog at the Institute. I was interested in what Cayce said about how he was able to help people. He would meet with the person asking for help. Somehow he knew what to prescribe for people who were sick or in pain. Sometimes he would even tell them how to find the remedy he recommended, even what store to look in.

Cayce believed our minds were timelessly connected. He'd enter a trance or sleep state, and in that state, he could access this combined universal mind, the mind that knows everything. All answers were available to him, and he answered people's questions that saved their lives. When he woke up from his trance, he had no recollection of anything that had happened, and no recollection of his advice to the person who had been seeking his help.

Reading how Cayce explained his work was a true moment of knowing for me. I felt the truth of his explanation of how he was able to help others. Cayce's explanation made sense to me, that we are all timelessly connected through the universal mind. Somehow, he was able, while in his trance, to access the mind that knows everything. I was very grateful to Kerry for telling me about Edgar Cayce and for suggesting I visit the Institute.

Another thing Kerry introduced into my life was the I Ching. This book is more than three thousand years old. It has been commonly used in China as an oracle, a way to predict the future.

Many people consult the book on New Year's Day or on their birthday. They want to find out what the future holds.

For me, it was never about predicting the future. I turned to the I Ching for words of wisdom, for answers to questions about my life. Everything I read in this book felt like it was coming from a place of deep understanding. The book always provided more meaning to my own situation, revealing things I may have sensed but hadn't yet brought to full awareness.

I asked the book about my relationships with people, my life, and what direction I might best take. I had lots to think about. Another name for the *I Ching* was *The Chinese Book of Changes*. It helped me to understand that everything is always changing and nothing stays still or the same.

Readers don't consult the *I Ching*, they "cast" it. In the beginning, I would cast the *I Ching* using pennies. Later I graduated to using old Chinese coins with a square hole in the middle. I liked the coins better. They felt more in keeping with the ancient book.

When working with the book, I knew I was supposed to try to wake up and be mindful. It was important to put my complete focus on my question.

The coins are thrown six times, and the result of each coin throw is recorded as a straight or broken line. The person ends up with a series of six lines called a hexagram. The book is divided into small essays, each corresponding to a hexagram. The hexagram essays have powerful titles like "Converting the Maiden," or "Persevering Favors."

I would hold the coins in my hand loosely and shake them. Shaking the coins felt like shuffling a deck of cards, refreshing their energy. Then I would drop the coins onto the table.

Ultimately, I abandoned the Chinese coins and made myself a set of yarrow stalks. This seemed to be the most ancient and traditional way of casting the *I Ching*.

The yarrow plant has yellow flowers on very straight sticks that don't bend easily. It grows everywhere I have ever lived.

I would arrange and rearrange the yarrow stalks into piles, in an ancient and precisely described way until I had my hexagram. I loved feeling that I was doing something ancient, something going back thousands of years. And it was something done by thousands of people before me, all of whom I imagined would have been searching as I was, looking for the best way forward.

Moments of Knowing

Kerry taught me boats, he showed me how to arrange a living space to be harmonious and peaceful, and he led me toward a number of spiritual practices and discoveries. During the next few years, Kerry and I sailed thousands of miles together. With Kerry, I was out in the sun on sparkling waters. I experienced nature in new ways. I traveled the seas and came ashore on sandy beaches. My relationship with Kerry opened me to many new experiences. He changed my life in many good ways.

Smuggling

Kerry had childhood friends in South Philly: Robby, Murray, and Lorenzo. The three of them were Jewish boys like Kerry. Robby was a natural born leader and the others had looked up to him since they were kids. He was tall, dark, and smart.

Murray was Robby's foremost follower, trusting Robby in all things, devoted to him throughout life. Murray was an all-around medium kind of guy. He was medium tall, medium attractive, and medium smart. He was friendly and comfortable to be around.

Lorenzo was a guy with an edge. He had a sharp face, somewhat pockmarked from teenage acne, and on him, it was somehow attractive. He looked like he had survived something that made him strong and different. From when I first met him, I thought Lorenzo was the coolest dude who had ever lived. He was completely unapproachable, perfect to admire from afar. He was a street pot dealer.

While Kerry had been a merchant marine for at least ten years, out at sea manning large tankers and container ships, these three longtime friends had settled in South Philly where they grew up. They had families, day jobs, and row houses on the same blocks where their parents lived. South Philly was mostly residential and mostly populated by conservative Italians and a sprinkling of Jews, which included these four friends.

Moments of Knowing

Robby and Murray worked as electricians, and they were bored. The group had a friend from Florida named Joe Block. He was a fit, strong person, and highly adventurous. He took a small rowboat around Cuba, traveling about 450 miles from Miami to Montego Bay, Jamaica. The trip took him about ten days. Joe rowed the boat back to Miami filled with pot. He knew some deserted beaches and had found a good landing spot where he left his car. He docked the boat, piled all the pot into his car, and drove to Philly to sell it to Lorenzo.

Joe made a huge profit. Although he was not from South Philly, Joe was a longtime and trusted friend of Kerry and the other South Philly friends. For the neighborhood guys, hearing the tale of Joe Block's adventure had them considering new, more exciting, and much wealthier lives.

They went into business together, Joe Block, Kerry, and the three South Philly guys. Kerry and Joe had boating skills. They mapped out how they could repeat Joe's profitable venture on a larger scale. The two of them made the first trip. They rented a thirty-foot sailboat in Miami and sailed it to Montego Bay, Jamaica.

In Jamaica, Joe had contacts—trusted relationships—for pot. The two guys filled the entire boat with bales of pot, and then sailed it back to Miami. The bales were loaded into a rented Winnebago and the rented boat was aired out and made immaculate for return to its owner. The Winnebago trip north to Philly took a little more than twenty-four hours. Lorenzo was waiting to receive the pot into his street dealer business. This trip was a pilot. Kerry and Joe repeated it a number of times, bringing along Murray and Robby as they got the details down. When the pot got to Philly, Lorenzo sold it.

By the time I met them, the guys had done the trip successfully many times. They had already made a small fortune.

Smuggling

Together they bought a downtown bar and called it Aphrodite. The bar was on one of Philadelphia's charming narrow streets, well located just a block or two from the center of town. Aphrodite was *the* place to be in Philly during the 1970s. The young Bruce Springsteen had his first drink at the Aphrodite bar. Some years later, it was described as "Studio 54 before there was Studio 54."

The guys now drove Mercedes. They organized and paid for junkets to Vegas with ten or twenty friends. They moved into larger homes. They stayed good friends.

Kerry recruited me to be part of this group. I was a little afraid, as I had never done anything illegal before. Living outside the law seemed scary to me, always wondering if I might be arrested. But I was a hippie, and clearly the law was wrong about pot. This wasn't a crime; this was civil disobedience. Morally, I felt I was on strong ground. And the excitement was as important as the principles. The lure of adventure was strong.

Kerry and I made many trips over the next few years, sometimes with Joe Block, sometimes with Murray. Robby was the mastermind, and after his initial trips, he didn't participate further on an actual sailboat. I made my first trip with Kerry and Murray. As soon as we got home, I was told to show up at the Aphrodite, where Robby handed me five thousand dollars. In hundreds, in a big pile. Like they were singles.

Robby said I had done well, and he offered me a new career. My job would be to cook for everyone on the boat, share in raising and lowering sails, help sail the boat in all conditions, including going up on the narrow foredeck to change sails when the boat was rocking up and down violently in a storm, take watches with everyone else, and in general, be a full crew member as well as the cook. I knew there would be plenty of time to relax, sunbathe, and watch the turtles swim by. So I said, "yes." My experiences at Kelly Girl and in business offices were not anything I ever wanted to pursue. I hated dressing for office work, having to wear stockings and the torture device of a girdle. Working with this group meant I no longer had to do office work. Life would be as exciting as it was meant to be.

I was able to realize a few dreams. I didn't have to go to work every day. My sailing trips came around only every two or three months, so I was able to go to art school, attending regularly whenever I was home.

The round trip from Miami to Jamaica took two weeks. We would depart Miami, sailing due east to the Bahamas. Bimini, the island closest to Miami was less than a sixty-mile trip. A sailboat usually cruised at about five knots, so it took us just twelve hours to reach Bimini. When we turned to the southeast, we sailed down the whole Bahamas island chain for six hundred miles. Then, about four days after leaving Miami, we entered the Windward Passage and sailed into the blue-green Caribbean. The last leg of the trip was a three-day cruise to Montego Bay. One way, Miami to Montego, was about a week on the water.

As was the practice on most small boat voyages, we divided our twenty-four-hour days into six four-hour watches, rotating as each of us took a turn on watch. When a crew member was on watch, they were in full charge of the boat, sitting at the wheel and keeping the boat on course. Because we split watch time evenly among us, everyone had the same amount of time when they needed to be responsible, alert, and aware. Everyone also has the same amount of time when they could forget all about the boat and sunbathe or go to sleep.

One night when I was on watch, everyone else on the boat was asleep. It was my first time being fully in charge of the boat. Kerry had trained me well, and I felt confident. The job was to know that we were headed in a safe direction—no rocks or land in front of us. I could either look at the compass needle, making sure I was always steering the course Kerry had given me, or once I was comfortably on course, I could steer by a star.

I loved steering by a star, just the very name of the process sounded magical. First, I would make sure I was on course by looking at the compass and seeing that the compass needle pointed to the course Kerry had given me. Then I would visually line up a rope or a wire or any small part of the boat with a bright star in the sky. My job was to keep this small part of the boat visually in the same line as the star—from my eye, up to the small part of the boat, then out to the star. One straight line. As long as I kept this small part of the boat lined up with my object in the sky, I knew I was on course.

Steering by a star was much easier than continually looking at the compass. As long as we were on course, there was rarely anything for me to do. Chocolate bars became the most exciting part of my watch. They were great for keeping me awake.

I considered myself a city girl. I had never experienced the power and beauty of nature. On the boat in the night, I was a small person in the center of a great circle of dark waters, bounded only by a circular horizon. There was nothing but me, the boat, and the water. Steering by a star made a connection with the sky that I could almost see, like a leash from heaven that pulled us in the right direction. I was at one with the ocean, which was all I could see in every horizontal direction. It was all there was.

The ocean had moods, colors, textures, and danger. It could be calm, or it could be disturbed. Sometimes it would flash with reflected starlight or moonlight. There were always unique patterns dancing across the water surface. Sometimes the water movement gained strength and power, moving up the scale toward danger. It could get so bad that it seemed Mother Nature wanted to kill us.

The first time I went through the Windward Passage, it was dawn. I had drawn the 4:00 to 8:00 a.m. watch, so everyone else was still asleep down below. I was sailing the boat ahead of a fresh breeze, the wind coming from behind, so the boat stayed flat without heeling over to one side. It was a comfortable way to sail, and I felt excited and easygoing at the same time. Looming close by and high on my right was Cuba. To my left in the east was the island of Hispaniola, far enough away so that it was only a dark, jagged silhouette. As the sun rose over that island, the dawn light was silver and pink on the waters around me.

The eastern-most point of Cuba, Punta de Maisi, ends in green cliffs hundreds of feet high. These cliffs loomed on my right. The cliffs host what they call the doctor winds, named for their supposedly healthful properties. The doctor winds were small white storm clouds blowing down the cliffs and swirling out to sea. They made vertical white stripes of cloud against the green cliffs as they descended to the ocean.

These boat trips were my first experience of nature close-up, sometimes beautiful like the Windward Passage and sometimes frightening. Nature changed everything about my experience of the moment, whichever way things were going. If nature was friendly, I felt calm and relaxed. If nature were dangerous, everything was tense and anxious.

I was terrified the first time we rendezvoused with another boat at sea, a mile or two off the coast of Montego Bay in the darkness of midnight. We were meeting the other boat so that pot could be transferred from their boat to ours. I felt vulnerable being the only woman on board, so I dressed to look like a boy, wearing a large, hooded, foul-weather jacket, hoping no one would notice. I stood on the far side of the deck, as far as possible from the men on the other boat. I was behind various stuff on our boat that might help to hide me, some vertical poles, and the big, wooden mainsail boom.

My heart pounded. I hadn't been this scared—ever. Who would be on this boat we were meeting? What might they do to us if they decided to steal and keep the valuable marijuana? Who would be the wiser, out here in the vast black sea?

Soon, five strong, large guys were throwing fifty-pound burlap bags from their boat onto our deck. Kerry and Murray grabbed the rough sacks as they hit our deck, then threw them below. There were fifty bags, twenty-five-hundred pounds in total. The street value of pot was about $500 a pound back then, so we were getting goods worth over a million dollars.

As I write this, I am astonished that I never realized the value of our cargo back then. I was getting my $5000, which was my focus. I never did the math. I never realized the stakes were so high.

We knew we were vulnerable to an enterprising thief. As soon as the other boat left, we knew we needed to leave immediately. The overstuffed burlap bags had to be arranged in the cabin below, quickly, and in a certain way so that every bag would fit. Kerry and Murray were experienced. By the time the other boat left, half the bags were already put away.

Kerry said, "We should leave right away. The sea is calm tonight, and the remaining cargo on deck is safe enough. I'll feel better once we're sure we're alone."

Murray and I agreed. We left everything lying on the deck and motored due west toward Mexico. After a couple of hours, there was no sign of anyone following us.

"Let's get the rest put away," said Kerry. We stopped again and got every fifty-pound bag stowed properly below. From outside the boat, we now looked like normal vacationers.

Moments of Knowing

For the duration of this weeklong return trip, the entire cabin was filled with these burlap bags of pot. There was just enough room below the ceiling for us to crawl over the bags. We slept on the bags. They were our floor, chairs, and table. Mostly, we stayed on deck and avoided going below, not wanting to deal with it. It was hard to get around, especially if the boat was rocking. I could never get used to the crushing smell of marijuana. Its pungency was so strong that it overwhelmed every sense. It was hard to breathe, hard to think. We never smoked pot. We were at work.

There was at least one big storm on every trip. During these storms, the entire crew would be forced to stay below for a day or two. First, we would hoist up a tiny storm sail that would keep us safely headed into the wind. Then, we would go below. We locked every porthole and battened down every hatch. Now we had no choice but to find a burlap bag seat, dine on a bag, and crawl over bags to get to the head. We could no longer go up on deck to escape the bulky bundles and their overpowering odor. The bags had been arranged in such a way as to leave the galley open, so I still could do my job as cook.

Storms were terrifying. Sticking my head out the main hatch, I could see waves towering over us, thirty feet high or more. The boat would climb up the closest wave, tilt over the top, and then slide fast down the other side. I stopped looking outside. I didn't get seasick, but looking at the gigantic waves was too frightening. I could just imagine one of them hitting us the wrong way.

In the cabin everything was always shaking. Anything that could fly around, flew around. We were careful to stow tins of food behind cabinet doors that closed tight, as well as anything else that might escape and hit one of us in the head.

Objects that could make a sound went into overdrive. The

Smuggling

symphony of the standing rigging banging against the masts went on for days. I associated the sound with my fear of the storm, but it lasted so long that my fear went away before the storm ended. I was very surprised when I discovered an important fact about how fear worked, at least for me. When I found myself in a terrifying situation, and when that situation lasted long enough, it became normal and no longer frightening. I experienced this more than once. It seemed that this might be an explanation for how people learn to live in all kinds of frightening situations. Fear had a time limit.

When a storm ended, it was heavenly. I'd wake up to the peacefulness of a normal day. I'd make coffee and not worry about the stove flipping upside down. Normal days often included a giant sea turtle swimming by or a school of dolphins at play coming to visit us.

The dolphins would swim alongside our boat on either side, then cross over one another at the bow. They played this game for an hour or two. I never tired of lying down on the deck at the bow, with my head stuck out over the water to watch them. The dolphins whistled to me as they zoomed by. I felt close to these creatures of the wild ocean, another new connection with nature.

We never ran aground, but we came close.

When we got too close to land, the sound of surf gave us plenty of warning. The trick was to back out exactly the way we came in. That way, we knew we wouldn't run aground.

Generally, we sailed along safely in deep water. But we had to go around the entire island of Cuba to get back to Miami, and any bad math could have us coming in too close to shore.

Moments of Knowing

We were lucky that we never ran aground. Being caught in Cuba would have meant jail time, possibly even decades in a Cuban prison.

Although we never ran aground, we did have a shipwreck. We were lucky that it took place before the boat was loaded with pot. We were in an empty boat on the way to Jamaica. We stopped in Nassau harbor to spend a day and enjoy the fun tourist town in the Bahamas.

We arrived at the island later than planned, and it was getting dark. Making landfall in the dark was always an iffy thing, and we should have waited until morning. But Kerry, Murray, and I were sick of the boat and wanted to get off for a while and walk around on solid ground. There would be a fancy hotel where we could stay for a night or two, some nice restaurants, and good shopping. We let these thoughts override our better judgment.

The Nassau guidebook we had on board indicated a typical aid to landing in the dark. The book instructed us to look on the hill behind the entry channel for two large matching red lights. One light would be higher than the other. These lights were supposed to be the largest red lights around, and it was supposed to be easy to align them one above the other. As long as we steered to keep these two lights in vertical alignment, we would be on track to sail safely into the harbor.

Unfortunately, there were hundreds of red lights on that hill. We made our best guess of which two lights we were supposed to align. In the middle of our alignment efforts, our engine failed. Suddenly we had no control of the boat. The surf caught us and pulled us rapidly toward a thirty-foot high breakwater of huge black boulders. All we could do was watch as the rocks came closer and closer.

Even though I was frozen with fear, I did what was asked of me, almost like a robot. Grab your passport. Tuck it into your underpants. Get on the radio and send out SOS Mayday calls in case anyone, anywhere was listening. I marched myself through every request from Kerry and Murray. The three of us were busy making the most of the few remaining minutes we had.

The boat hit the rocks. The surf had us in a relentless grip. It pounded us onto the rocks over and over. The boat crashed sideways, its full length slamming into the rocks. After each crash, the surf would push us back out to sea a few feet, then sweep us in again for the next crash. The sounds were violent. The boat started to splinter. The surf was determined to beat this beautiful forty-two-foot sailboat into small sticks. We had to get off.

Each of us, one at a time, had to stand up on the edge of the boat and leap onto the rocks at just the right moment, when the boat was slamming toward the rocks. If we jumped too soon and got caught in the water, we could be smashed by the boat. If we jumped too late, the distance might be too far, and we might be lost in the waves and the water.

Both guys jumped successfully as I watched. Then they coached me. When it was my turn, I stood on the four-inch wide, shiny, wooden gunnel that was the edge of the boat. With one hand, I hung onto some rigging within reach, a sturdy metal wire. Murray and Kerry were right there, only six feet away from me, both safely out of the water, completely focused on getting me to safety. They were mentally helping me to take the leap.

"Now!" they screamed. I let go and jumped off the boat.

I made it onto the rocks. I scrambled up quickly before the boat returned with its next crash. Murray and Kerry jumped down and grabbed my arms and helped me to reach safety.

I was thrilled to have made it off the boat. We climbed the rocks, up and up. Finally, we reached the top of the breakwater. We sat down on the topmost rocks, our backs to the ocean, looking over a peaceful channel and hoping that rescue might come soon. No one was hurt or in any pain.

Four or five hours later, I noticed that my index finger was not where it was supposed to be. It had become dislocated when I jumped, and the finger was sitting high up on the back of my hand. I believe this would normally have been quite painful, but in the excitement, I hadn't even noticed it. I never felt any pain. I guess my body was just too busy with the entire experience to worry about a finger.

At dawn, a boat of local volunteer rescue workers motored up the channel toward us. We jumped up and down and waved. Part of their twenty-four-hour-a-day program was to monitor for SOS signals, and they had heard ours. They were kind and sympathetic, people who could understand what we had just been through. They gave us vodka and blankets. Finally, we were safe. I had narrowly escaped a bad end. I was not quite the same person I had been that morning.

We came back later that day, walking out on the top of the breakwater to where we had spent the night. We wanted to see the entire scene in daylight and understand just where we had been. On our left was the calm and friendly channel. On our right, the sea still pounded endlessly, as it probably is today. The boat was gone. Washed higher up on the rocks were some scraps of wood and one bright purple knee sock. I never wore purple knee socks again.

Although the guys continued importing pot for some years, that was the end of my smuggling career. I didn't want the danger. I didn't want to live on the outskirts of society, and I didn't want to be a criminal.

Just in case any law enforcement agents are reading this chapter, I assure you that this was completely fiction. Everyone can dream, can't they?

Island of
the Red Hood

In the 1970s, when I was in my early thirties, I moved into a group house in Philadelphia with a number of good friends. It was similar to the house owned by The Big Eagle where I had lived in after my divorce. This new house was just a number of friends moving in together.

For unknown reasons, we called the place Bumfuck Egypt. I had been looking for a place to live and was very happy when I was invited to join these friends. I was teaching for Head Start, and no longer involved in any aspects of my previous less-than-legal ways of earning a living.

There was one person living in our new house whom I hadn't met before. His name was Michael, and he was a friend of a friend. He and I hit it off immediately. He was handsome, blond, and easy-going. Michael was fun, and he loved exploring ideas, theories, and far-out stories and happenings. And he was just enough taller than me to make me happy. I was smitten.

Michael was from a well-known Philadelphia family that had endowed him with more money than he knew what to do with. He even owned a small Picasso. The two of us would stay up late with our housemates, talking about everything and listening to the ambient new age sounds of *Hearts of Space* on the radio. My kinda music. Michael and I decided to share a room, developing our relationship further, and halving our rent.

I was working in a leather store owned by a friend. He made lots of bags, but he also wanted to sell leather clothing. I had developed strong sewing skills over the years. I knew how to make leather ponchos, pants, vests, etc. I worked a few days a week, without a fixed schedule. It was a great job for me, where I made my own time and created things both useful and beautiful. I didn't feel tied to the job; it felt good that I could move on whenever I wanted to.

After about a year, we heard from Michael's friend, Robert Goodyear. Robert was starting a hippie commune in West Virginia. He had purchased ten acres on top of a mountain and named it, "The Island of the Red Hood," because there was an old red hood of a car lying in the front yard. Robert was living there with his long-time girlfriend, a potter, and he invited us to move there. Michael and I packed up and went.

The commune was half an hour's drive from the tiny town of Hinton, near the middle of the state. I had only lived in large East Coast cities, never in a rural area. The primary structure on the property was a hundred-year-old log cabin. Each log was more than a foot high and a foot wide. The first floor had a living room and a big kitchen, and there were two bedrooms upstairs.

The front door opened into the big living room. An ornate, antique, wood-burning stove was made of black metal and put out enough heat to keep the entire cabin warm, including the kitchen and the entire second floor. The stove looked like a little round soldier, with an elaborate military headdress. Robert and his girlfriend lived in one of the second-floor bedrooms, and Michael and I moved into the other.

Soon, two wonderful women from Canada arrived. I immediately liked them. They were easy to get along with and fun. One of these women eventually became Robert's girlfriend, ending his long-standing relationship with his potter girlfriend.

Our group had considerable skill in crafts. I had worked in the leather store in the city, sewing custom leather and suede clothing like vests, ponchos, and jackets. The Canadian women were excellent seamstresses as well. They created beautiful designs that combined embroidery with leather work. Sleeves to a leather top might be attached to the bodice by two inches of colorful, decorative stitchery. This was a design feature I had never seen before and immediately loved. The contrast between the heavy leather or suede with the delicate embroidery was dramatic.

We converted the five or six outbuildings into craft workshops. One became the leather studio. I had brought my sewing machine, as had others. Among us, we had all the tools needed to cut and sew leather clothing.

Robert's old girlfriend took over another of the outbuildings, creating a pottery shop complete with a potter's wheel, kiln, and everything needed to make pots. An English woman named Jenny arrived. She was a skilled batik artist, and she converted yet a third outbuilding into a batik studio. I often visited her studio, learning to work with the fabrics and dyes, applying wax resist patterns with a Tjanting.

A Tjanting is used for the precise application of hot wax. Once the wax cools on the fabric, the piece is dipped into a new color of dye. Since the dye cannot penetrate the waxed areas, beautiful designs are built up from repeated applications of wax followed by different colors of dye.

A well-known gallery in downtown Philadelphia took an interest in the clothing and craft objects we created at The Island of the Red Hood. The owners invited us to have our own Island of the Red Hood show at their gallery. Each year, the show was stocked with new and different creations.

I loved our life on the farm. My days were my own. I didn't have to spend hours at some job in which I had no interest. Michael was able to support the two of us without any trouble, paying into the commune funds more than enough to cover the two of us and several others, as well. Finances among the group were informal, with each person supposedly contributing enough to cover their own needs.

Some months after her arrival, Jenny's father came over from England. He had gardening skills beyond any of us, and right away he planted an enormous vegetable garden. I loved walking through the rows of plants and later, gathering vegetables for dinner. My cat, Boudreaux, would always come into the garden with me. Boudreaux was supposed to be an indoor cat, but he would spend every indoor minute waiting to dash out as soon as the door opened. He was obsessed with going outside.

One time there was a total eclipse of the moon. For some reason, all the women and none of the men were drawn to gather together outside to watch the eclipse. A little song started among us. It quickly turned into a kind of howling at the moon. With dancing. We watched the black shadow of the earth cut into the white circle of the moon, move all the way across, and finally slide off.

～

Michael had been childhood friends with singer Arlo Guthrie. One time Arlo came to visit us. He sang for everyone, and it was exciting to meet someone famous and realize he was also simply a nice guy. I still love the song, "Alice's Restaurant."

Island of the Red Hood

One day, the three of us walked in the woods together. We were all surprised to smell witch hazel. We didn't know that fragrant witch hazel bushes grew naturally in the West Virginia woods. I didn't even know it came from a plant.

At the commune, we did a lot of LSD. I had always been just a social drug user. I smoked pot or did acid to be with other people who were doing it. I was more interested in the communication than in the high. Michael could drive a car on acid, which was completely unimaginable to me. For me, driving a car on acid would have been like flying a 747. Although we did acid and smoked pot, no one did any other drugs. No escapism, strictly mind expansion, or so we told ourselves. We were a middle-class bunch. In contrast to preconceptions about hippie communes, there was no wild sex or much of anything wild other than the LSD.

After a year, the population at Island of the Red Hood reached its height at about fifteen people. Most everyone lived in various outbuildings that we hadn't been using. Everyone gathered for meals.

After dinner in the evenings, we listened to record albums. Led Zeppelin was a big favorite. Everyone played along with the music. At least one person had a guitar, someone else had a flute, and others sang with the band. I always played spoons. Some people just slapped their hands on their thighs. We would make music together for hours every evening.

When we did drugs together, fifteen turned out to be a lot of people doing acid at one time in a small space. People would be in the main room together near the little wooden stove. I remember someone brought Tabitha, the goat, into the main room. She climbed up on the couch next to me and sat there peacefully. Under the influence of the LSD, I felt quite close to her, as if she were a long-lost relative or lifetime friend.

Moments of Knowing

Another time on acid, we all went for a walk to see the sunrise, and there was Tabitha down the road. Perhaps she picked up on our unusual LSD energy because she began to run up the road toward us at top speed. Michael stepped into her path with his arms stretched out, and Tabitha stopped right in front of him. The sun was just coming up behind the two of them, streaking the sky with pastel colors and bright gold. On acid, everything had many levels of symbolism. At this moment, our new day equated to a new start in life. I didn't yet know how much I would need that new start.

We had four black-and-white possibly sheepdogs and also a chestnut horse. Various people took responsibility for various animals. Others gravitated to other chores. I spent much of my time in the kitchen with a small group of four or five who liked cooking. We made meals for fifteen. I would go food shopping in Hinton and fill up five grocery carts, enough food for a week.

There was only one neighboring house, about a twenty-minute walk away. An older couple lived there, and they were friendly to us. They gave us eggs from their chickens. One day, I cracked open an egg, and it had no yolk. I jumped back from the table, frightened. I took it as a bad omen. I believed it meant I would have no children.

That turned out to be the case. I don't regret it today, but at the time, it seemed scary.

A woman from the Midwest moved into the commune. She seemed wholesome and healthy, the epitome of the American Midwest. Michael fell for her. He moved out of our room in the log cabin and into her tent in the woods. I was devastated. I contrasted myself with her unfavorably, with my so-so health habits and my more intellectual Jewish background as compared with her seemingly more wholesome midwestern approach to life. I remember going out to the garden one night,

Island of the Red Hood

Boudreaux following me. I felt so sad standing in the darkness in a place where I had previously felt such happiness. I hurt all over, inside and out. Something had to change.

There in the dark garden, I decided I would leave the next day. One of the commune residents had borrowed and wrecked my red Volvo, so I would have to hitchhike.

The next morning, I packed a small day pack with my tarot cards and my sandals. What else could I possibly need? I didn't say goodbye to anyone, I just took off through the woods. The four dogs came with me. I worried about them, but eventually they turned back and left me to walk on alone. I made it to the big highway and hitched back to Philly. It felt like everything was ending. But it turned out to be a new start.

My First Job

Back in Philadelphia, my best friend Sylvia had gotten a job with a local office of the Pennsylvania Department of Welfare. Like me, she had been a humanities major in college. Neither of us had any vocational skills. It was well-known among local college grads that you could get a job with the Department of Welfare without any skills or experience, as long as you had the college degree.

To apply for the job, I had to take a test. I remember this test as being ridiculously easy, with questions like the following:

Your client has lost his temper and is yelling at you. You would:

Yell back at the client.

Calmly reassure the client and explain any issues.

Hit the client.

Leave the room immediately.

Not surprisingly, I got the job. It was 1977, and I was thirty-four years old. I had managed to avoid getting a "real job" for my entire adult life up to this time. But my attitude had changed. I called it "joining the world." I wanted to get credit cards and not have to worry about being arrested or going to jail.

My new job started with a six-week training program where I learned how to be an Income Maintenance Worker II, job-title-speak for a person who checks if people are still eligible to get their welfare checks. We were more commonly known as caseworkers. After the training, I was assigned to one of the many welfare offices in the city, in my case the Passyunk office in South Philly. South Philly was a racially mixed, lower-middle-class neighborhood. There were blocks inhabited only by Italian families, alternating with blocks where only people of color lived. Strong racial tensions existed between local Italians and Blacks. I had never encountered this kind of racism before, growing up in an all-white suburb where there were no people of color at all. I was only in South Philly during daylight hours, but I had heard that Blacks who dared to walk on the local Italian streets after dark might be taught a violent lesson.

Our office was on Passyunk Avenue, pronounced "Pass-shunk." The name is Native American, a Leni Lenape tribal word meaning "in the valley." I'm not sure where the valley had been because by then it was just a big-city neighborhood.

Our small, two-story office building had once housed a funeral home. The basement had restrooms and break rooms where employees could relax. The first floor had a two-woman reception desk that faced seating for about thirty clients awaiting appointments. The place had the creepy smell of formaldehyde.

Fifty caseworkers had desks in the one large room that made up the second floor of the building. The room was more than two hundred feet in length. Each of us had an ugly gray metal desk about seven feet wide with file drawers on both sides. Our fifty desks were arranged in two long rows, half the desks facing the other half. Each of us had a coworker directly across and a neighbor on either side. The fifty of us were assigned to eight supervisors, each of whom had a private window office around the edges of the big room.

Welfare recipients received State of Pennsylvania welfare checks twice a month as well as federal food stamps once a month. It was our job to monitor these people. We had a file for each individual or family, and we checked twice yearly that they were still eligible for assistance. Each worker was given about three hundred cases. Since there were fifty workers, there were about fifteen thousand welfare cases being managed from our office. Each of my three hundred cases came with a huge file. The largest files covered a large family that may have been on welfare for many generations. Files could bulge up to more than two inches thick.

I had two afternoons of field time a week, during which I was required to physically visit the homes of nine or ten families. Over the course of a year, I visited every one of my cases twice, my two visits about six months apart. All my families lived in abject poverty, with the barest minimum of furniture and nothing decorative. The children were always present so that we could count them and confirm they were still at home and eligible for assistance. Most families were pleasant and accommodating, if a little frightened since their income was on the line. We were warned never to sit on any furniture in case it had bugs crawling in it. Visits were not lengthy.

After each visit, there were about twenty pages of paperwork to complete during the following days back at the office. This included forms to be filled out and narratives to be written, everything to document the status of the family at the time of the visit. Single mothers with children were automatically supported by the Aid to Dependent Children program, but if a father was present, the mother and children were no longer eligible. For this reason, fathers never appeared during home visits and had no official existence in our records.

Today, I can see that this rule damaged the stability of marriage for thousands of families receiving welfare.

Filling out the many forms was an exercise in knowing

the latest requirements. One week a certain field had to filled in with just the right buzz word, and a few weeks later that field was no longer important and some other field was queen for a day. We caseworkers heard from one another, via gossip channels, what was best for us to put on the forms. There was never anything official, and we never knew anything about why the importance of information varied as it did. Perhaps the information was distantly related to legislation or news. All we knew was that if you didn't get the right buzz words in the right place on the form, it would get bounced back. I hated to see my work returned to me. I was already done with the previous week's cases, and now here was one of them, back on my desk.

During the week after a home visit, I updated the family file and then turned it over to my supervisor, Alicia Minton. Alicia was a smart woman. She enjoyed her power over her six workers. Her favorite expression was, "I live in the real world." This somewhat jaded comment arose whenever a worker tried to make a client seem more eligible than they might actually be.

My experience of my fellow welfare workers was that they were a kindhearted bunch who wanted to help the families in their caseloads. There was a stereotype that welfare workers were critical and mean, and they wanted to get people off welfare, but I never saw any evidence of it. With few exceptions, welfare workers seemed compassionate and understanding toward their clients.

Alice reviewed everything I did. If she was annoyed with me for any reason, such as my being late to work or taking a long lunch break, I might get all my files back on my desk immediately, with picky changes requested. But if I were in Alice's good graces, she would call me in for a quick review, and all my files would be approved and passed on to downstairs. "Downstairs" issued checks to recipients, but I never understood any of the details of what they did or how they did it.

The first downstairs room was called Masterfile. Masterfile was a large room inhabited 100 percent by women. I didn't know what their work was, but from the name, I assumed they did some kind of filing. What interested me was that they had a fax machine. This was the latest in technology, and I had never seen one before. It was so exciting to see this new machine at work. I would walk into Masterfile and pay my respects to the fax machine and all it stood for in the future of office machines.

There was a certain way I had learned to behave in Masterfile if I wanted them to actually handle my work. Other more experienced caseworkers had given me precise instructions. I should walk over and stand silently a few feet away from the desk of the Masterfile person I wanted to speak with. Sometimes it was a long wait. I spent the time hoping they would notice me and invite me to speak. Standing and waiting for recognition was protocol. Even clearing one's throat was frowned upon. I had never before seen this unique office protocol, and I have never seen it again since.

Everyone in Masterfile seemed to resent me and to enjoy my being forced to wait silently for long periods of time. Perhaps they resented all the caseworkers from upstairs. I don't know if there was racial motivation since many caseworkers were white and most Masterfile workers were Black, but it was likely. Our office included institutionalized, racial animosity between various groups.

After a successful visit to Masterfile, documents went to the other downstairs room, which was called RAN. I don't know what RAN meant or what they did. They may have controlled the money. I knew that they wrote the checks. No one in RAN was pleasant, just like in Masterfile.

My First Job

Each case folder would leave my desk with a routing slip stapled to the file folder. This label had rows where I could write in all the stops the file needed to make before coming back to me: "Supervisor, Masterfile, RAN," was the usual. I started doing artwork on the routing slips. I did portraits of some of my coworkers in pale white-out, green-out, and blue-out, so someone could still read the routing information. People liked the portraits of themselves superimposed over a bureaucratic form that represented their daily work. Everyone knew not to let Alicia Minton or any other supervisors see their portraits. It was fun doing these portraits, and it made the workday a little less boring.

I have a framed routing slip hanging on the wall in our kitchen today, a portrait of my husband, Stuart. Yes, I met him at Welfare.

I felt reasonably comfortable with the job and my coworkers. I didn't mind visiting my clients and writing up their situations. The job worked for me, and I stayed there for three years.

There were housing projects close to the office, and almost everyone who lived in the projects was on welfare through our office. There were low-rise projects, such as the Passyunk Homes, with one-story houses. These low-rise housing projects were dangerous and unpleasant places to live or visit. Crime rates were high, and trash blew about the streets and the yards. Interactions with passing residents on the street were not friendly.

There was also a high-rise project nearby, the Taylor Home. This building was about thirty stories high, a nightmarish place to live or even to visit. The elevators didn't work. As one climbed up thirty flights of stairs, one would stumble over drunks collapsed in the stairwells and inhale unidentifiable foul odors. Anyone might be lying in wait to attack. Women were not required to visit clients in the high-rise projects, and it was scary for the men.

Working for the welfare department changed me. Seeing the difficulties faced by my impoverished clients made me determined to find a career that would pay me well. It just needed to be legal.

The Man
of My Dreams

I met the man I would later marry at the welfare office in Philadelphia. Stuart's desk was not directly across from mine, but it was only one down, so we faced one another diagonally. He had a number of toys on his desk, rubber duckies and little stuffed animals. But the real glory on his desk was a stack of used staples about eight inches high. I imagined that thousands of staples had gone into this little tower of metal. I had never seen a stack of staples—before or since.

Each week, like the rest of us, Stu would take out his five or six giant files for the families he planned to visit, stacking them up on his desk for review. He opened each file and removed the documents. Over the years, caseworkers would attempt to organize a file, stapling pages into groups that made sense at the time. But after a number of years, files would inevitably become disorganized. Most of our client files were made up of haphazardly stapled together piles of old and new documents mixed up in no intelligent order. They needed reorganization. Stu's files got exactly that.

First, he removed every staple from every piece of paper. The staples went into the desktop staple tower. Stuart then proceeded to organize the file chronologically so that it became an actual record of the family history on welfare rather than a large pile of random paper. Related documents were stapled together into meaningful groups.

By the time Stu completed a file, he might have removed twenty to fifty staples. These used staples went atop the growing monument on his desk. Stu had worked at Welfare for five or six years, so the pile was getting tall. The staples pile was Stu's monument to bureaucracy, disorganization, and the rarity of keeping good records for the thousands of families we served.

One day Stu invited me to go for coffee around the corner. I liked him. He was quite handsome, but better than that, he was warm, friendly, and easy to be with. He had a wonderful sense of humor. Blond, healthy, and fun, he had clear blue eyes that had seen a lot. He came from a well-off and accomplished family of professionals, his mother an architect and his father a PhD who taught at the medical school. Stu was the youngest of three, and both of his older siblings were professionally successful, one with IBM and the other with Xerox.

Stu was like me; he was more interested in life than in success. His parents didn't really get him. They didn't understand his own kind of subtle intelligence, and they supported his being traumatically left behind a grade when he was around fifteen. He and I shared a childhood where we weren't really seen for who we were. When I met him, Stu was finishing up his master's degree. Like me, he was ready to "join the world."

We went for coffee a few times a week for about a month. Then he invited me for a Scotch after work. It was 1978, so the bar he took me to had disco music and a spinning disco ball. We danced. We both ordered Johnny Walker Red on the rocks. After another month or so, Stu asked me out on a date.

I had moved to a nicer loft and had a wonderful new roommate, Sharon. She was getting her PhD in anatomy. We became close friends, and still are, a lifetime later. Stu came by more and more often.

One day, Sharon said to me, "He's the one. Don't fuck it up."

I had had a lot of boyfriends over the years, and Sharon knew that. I wasn't likely to fuck this one up, but Sharon wanted to make sure. She was right. He was the one. And I didn't fuck it up.

Stu moved into Center City Philadelphia, much closer to me than where he had lived before. We had a good time as a couple for about three years. Stu's siblings lived out West, his brother in Reno and his sister in California. Every year, the family and their friends went on a week-long backpacking trip near Yosemite. Stu had done a lot of hiking, but he hadn't yet been out West before deciding to join the backpack. The trip was life-changing for Stu. He wanted more.

After he returned from Yosemite, his brother invited him to move to Reno. The plan was that they would go into business together making hiking packs for cameras. QuickShot was the snappy business name. I understood Stu needed to get out of Philadelphia. He'd been there since he was born. He wanted to be closer to his siblings, and he was drawn to move to where there were new experiences and greater access to the outdoors.

We made plans for him to go first, then for me to follow in a few months. Stu drove across the country. He settled in Reno. For his job, he traveled all over the Southwest, getting to know the territory and introducing QuickShot to the area. We spoke on the phone, at length, every Sunday. Months went by. We didn't address my coming out West. Gradually, years went by. I spent all my vacations with him and was thrilled as Stu showed me around his new world. Yosemite opened my eyes to a new scale of grandeur in nature. The red rock of Arizona and New Mexico was breathtaking.

Moments of Knowing

More years went by. We still spoke every Sunday. Each of us tried dating other people, but those relationships went nowhere, mainly because our relationship with one another didn't allow us to commit to anyone else.

Twelve years later, I joined Stu. The years apart were valuable. Each of us was able to make changes that allowed us to be together. I spent those twelve years learning that I didn't *need* to be in a relationship. I was just fine by myself, and I was happy alone. I enjoyed my living space, pursued my passions of reading, writing, and painting, and became successful and skilled in my new computer science career. During those twelve years, I spent a lot of time in therapy, which changed my life even more. By the time I joined Stu, I knew I was choosing a new life with Stu, not *needing* a new life with Stu.

For Stu's part, my theory is that before our twelve years apart, he had what I call "commit-o-phobia," a common malady among the men of my generation. During our separation, Stu developed an interest in something deeper, an appreciation for a relationship with more depth, something lifelong. It's forty-five years since we met, and we're still having fun. And he's still the one.

Card Counting

In 1978, I was living in Philadelphia. Local residents were excited that casinos were coming to Atlantic City, only an hour away. Before this time, the only casinos in the United States were in Nevada. But now, there was so much interest in the upcoming advent of casinos that the *Philadelphia Inquirer* had started a regular gambling column, which I consistently read. Some months before the first Atlantic City casino opened, the newspaper ran a story about blackjack card counting. I had read about card counting, and I was interested.

I have always loved playing cards. When I was twelve, when I came to live with my father and Winnie, she summed it up by saying, "Great! Now we have a fourth for bridge." She taught me bridge, and I still enjoy playing it. Once I mastered the complicated game of bridge, all other card games were easy. I had played blackjack a little with friends. I knew the general idea of the game was to have your cards all add up to twenty-one, hence the game is also known as "21."

The way casinos make money is that every game they offer gives the casino a statistical advantage over the players. With blackjack, that advantage is about 1 percent. This means for every $1 people bet, they get 99 cents back. Whether they win or lose a particular hand, overall, they will lose one penny for every $1 they bet. If they bet $100, they will get back $99.

Moments of Knowing

Even if they win big sometimes, overall, they will always lose 1 percent of their money.

I had read that card counting could reverse this advantage. By counting cards, a player could have the advantage over the casino. Professors at MIT had run millions of hands of blackjack through a computer and proved that card counting worked. And a card-counting team of students and graduates from MIT won millions of dollars from the casinos, which was enough for me to believe it would work.

MIT math professor Ed Thorp is credited with the invention of card counting. I read his book, *Beat the Dealer*, in which he explained card counting and how to do it. Coincidentally, Ed lived in California, about a block away from my father. They lived on different streets, but they had the same street number (21, most appropriately). Ed and my dad would frequently get each other's mail, so they got to know one another. Life's coincidences seem important, don't they?

Looking back, I can see that my interest in card counting partly arose from my fear of ending up in a boring job and having a boring life. And from my love of adventure. I imagined I could make enough money counting cards to live without going to work every day, while having fun doing it.

I called the reporter who wrote the gambling column, Jerry Patterson. He was forming a card-counting team and was willing to train new members. I made an appointment to be interviewed for the team. It went well, and I was accepted.

Jerry had a blackjack table in his living room. There were four other members of the team. Jerry taught us to count cards. We played blackjack with imaginary money, and we kept close track of our imaginary winnings.

Card counting was not that hard for me. I didn't actually have to "count" the cards. I just had to remember a single number at all times. It's like a "temperature" number. It told me if the deck was "hot" or "cold." When the deck was hot, I would win more money, so I would bet high. When the deck was cold, I would lose more often, so I bet the minimum.

The first casino in Atlantic City was Resorts International. Stuart managed to learn card counting by some kind of mental osmosis. I had worked hard to learn how to do it, and I am still wondering how he so effortlessly grasped the concepts that I had spent hours practicing and learning. But he did. He soon became an honorary member of the team.

The job that Stuart and I had at the welfare office included field time twice a week. We could leave work at noon and complete our field work in an hour. It took another hour on the new Atlantic City Expressway, but by 2:00 p.m. we were in Atlantic City. A quick stop for a tuna sub at the famous White House Subs, and we were on our way.

The casinos were packed day and night with enthusiastic gamblers. The $2 table was most popular, and there was always a crowd of at least ten people waiting for one of the seven seats at the table to become available. Stu and I often waited over an hour, but eventually we were sitting at the table, playing blackjack and counting cards. And winning. Not every time. But more often than not.

Jerry Patterson found investors, and soon our team had a $40,000 bank to bet with. Our goal was to double it. It took us a few months, but we did it. My personal stake in the bank was only $1,000, but when we were done, I had $2,000, which was a lot of money. And I had never had so much fun making money.

It didn't take long for the casinos to catch on. While card counting is not illegal, the casinos can and will prohibit someone from playing. We learned about the "eye in the sky." Casino employees watched everything from up in the ceilings.

Moments of Knowing

We knew they were watching the blackjack players to see who was counting cards, and we knew they were onto us.

At Jerry's house, our team practiced looking like regular players who were not counting cards. Often, card counters concentrated so intensely, it was obvious. They didn't chat or socialize with the other players. They were stiff and overly focused on the game. They never took their eyes off the cards. It was obvious to casino employees that these players were not just out for an enjoyable time with a fun game.

Jerry taught us to chat while counting, look around with interest at everything that was going on, and engage with other players. It was intense for our team, keeping track of the all-important number for the count and also keeping track of other numbers representing other aspects of the game, such as how many aces had been played. We learned to count aces with our toes. It's just like counting with your fingers, only done with toes. While doing this internal math and counting, we learned to look relaxed and like we were having a good time.

Once we were seated at a table, a casino waitress brought us all the alcoholic drinks we wanted for free. No doubt the casinos knew that getting a little drunk might encourage losing a lot of money. Jerry told us to order continual free drinks and pretend to drink them, but to actually pour them out onto the probably already filthy industrial carpet under the table, without being seen.

For practice, while we were counting cards, we asked one another questions. Jerry pointed us toward especially hard questions, such as those with numbers in the answer, like "What's your birthday?" It's difficult to say numbers out loud and at the same time remember other numbers in your head. But that's what we learned to do. We learned to smile and look relaxed, just vacationers or workers on a day off, out for a fun time at the new casinos.

But even though we worked at looking relaxed, the casino knew we were counting. All they had to do was count along with us. They hired card counters who watched us from the eye in the sky. Just like us, these card counters knew when the deck got hot, and they saw that we raised our bet whenever that happened. Ipso facto: We were card counters.

One day I won $5,000 in five minutes. It was quite a thrill. I immediately worried that I would be thrown out of the casino, so I quit playing, grabbed my big pile of casino chip winnings, and threw them into my purse. I walked directly out the door onto the boardwalk, then walked up and down the beach for about half an hour. I hoped the dealer and pit boss employees who had seen me win would forget about me.

Finally, I went back into the casino. I walked up to the cashier's window to convert my $5,000 worth of chips into cash. I got my money and put it safely away in my purse, but within a minute, two casino employees appeared. They wore suits and ties, and there was one to my right and one to my left. Each had a hand on one of my elbows. They steered me off the casino floor, down the stairs into the basement, and into an empty office.

They said they knew I was card counting, and they took my photo. They also asked me for identification. I told them I didn't have any ID with me, but that my name was Mary Blaze. I always liked the name Mary Blaze. It suited my rebellious and adventuresome side.

By this time, two other casinos had opened in Atlantic City. I played in all three regularly. I presumed that Resorts International would circulate my photo and my name to the other casinos, but they didn't. I could never play at Resorts again, but I was happy to discover that I could still play at the two other casinos without any problem. Our team continued to win, and Stuart and I continued to enjoy ourselves.

After a year or two, Stu and I had played enough blackjack. We lost our fervor for the game. But even today, many years later, we still enjoy heading up to Reno once in a while, near where we now live, for an evening of card counting. We usually make enough money for an elegant dinner. Blackjack card counting was a fun activity for me. I was done with breaking the law. But I still enjoyed breaking the rules.

Gurdjieff
and Buddhism

During those twelve years when Stu and I were apart, I explored spiritual practice. What that really meant was I had a boyfriend who explored spiritual practice and at that point in my life, if my boyfriend was doing something, then I was doing it as well.

New boyfriend Thomas was in a Gurdjieff Group. George Gurdjieff was a Russian philosopher, mystic, and spiritual teacher. He lived from around 1870 through the mid-1900s. At the time of the Russian Revolution, about 1917, he gathered a group of spiritual seekers around himself, including the Russian pianist Thomas de Hartman, Olgivanna Lloyd Wright, the wife of Frank Lloyd Wright, and P.D. Ouspensky, the writer who recorded all of Gurdjieff's teachings.

Ouspensky's books are a complete guide to Gurdjieff's teachings.

Gurdjieff's stated mission was "to bring the wisdom of the East to the West." He taught the members of his group to practice mindfulness, calling it "self-remembering." He introduced the enneagram to the Western world, a nine-pointed star used to define personality types.

Moments of Knowing

Today, the enneagram has seen a resurgence in popularity through the work of Gurdjieff's students and others.

Gurdjieff trained some of his students to teach. One of his students founded the Fellowship of Friends, a Gurdjieff-type school centered at the Renaissance Winery in Marysville, California. Several thousand people belonged to the Fellowship, many of whom lived at the winery and helped to produce their well-respected wines. The Fellowship of Friends was a classic cult. It had a charismatic male leader who happened to be fabulously wealthy. As in many cults, this leader demanded absolute obedience, even including his deciding whom one should marry. There were frequent sex scandals involving the leader. He made end-of-the-world prophecies that didn't come true on schedule.

A Fellowship of Friends member named Mark came to Philadelphia to start his own Fourth Way school. He called it "Maxima," which, in Latin, meant the whole or the highest part of anything. I followed my aforementioned boyfriend and became a member of Maxima. After about six months of working with Mark, I moved into the Maxima teaching house. This was a beautiful old stone house in the suburbs of Philadelphia, with five bedrooms and four other students in residence. I wanted to work more closely with these other Maxima students on self-remembering.

This was my first exposure to mindfulness and its benefits. I realized I had discovered a wonderful practice that helped me to experience my life more deeply and to better know what I was doing. I took less for granted and appreciated more.

Mark was married to a woman named Rebecca. As time went by, Rebecca and I became close friends. Each Sunday afternoon, we had our Maxima meeting. Everyone sat in a circle in the teaching house living room, while Mark gave a talk and took questions. As I arrived for my first visit, I looked through a small window in the front door, and there I saw a print of my favorite painting in the world. I took this as a sign that I had come to the right place.

The painting was Leonardo da Vinci's *Annunciation*. The Archangel Gabriel had come to announce to Mary that she would bear the Christ Child. To me, this painting was never about the Christian symbolism of the virgin and the angel. To me, it had always symbolized the presence of the spiritual in my life. The archangel brought a moment of knowing. When a moment of knowing came to me, it felt just like the scene in the painting. An angel was speaking. And I was paying attention.

Later, I did my own collage of the *Annunciation*. I sit in an old SUV with Gabriel across from me. I loved Fra Angelico's Archangel Gabriel rather than Leonardo's because of the streams of color that Fra Angelico painted in Gabriel's wings.

Our group became close over time, practicing self-remembering together. It was always a wonderful practice, being present to what was happening in that very moment. At first, Mark was positive and inspiring. There was a photo of him from that time with a butterfly alighting on his shoulder. The photo summarized how I felt about him. He was light and spontaneous and *in the moment*. At the beginning.

One of my most memorable experiences in Maxima came after an entire day of Sufi dancing.

Sufi dancing is a form of meditation, unusual in that it is physically active meditation. It includes whirling, and most people have heard of "whirling dervishes." Sufi dancing practice goes back to the thirteenth century when the poet Rumi founded an order of dancers.

One of the Maxima members had practiced Sufi dancing, and she offered to share it with the group. Maxima rented a large hall for a day. I remember the light in the hall was dim, which felt right. Like most of the others, I had little experience in dancing and none at all in dancing as a meditative form. I was glad the dim light provided kind of a private space for me to try this new activity. I remember how much I enjoyed the dancing and the day. By afternoon, I felt just great, as if I had been meditating for hours. In contrast to sitting meditation, which was very calming and peaceful, I felt energized and excited, peaceful in a more active way.

When the dancing ended, I went outside. The bright light of daytime seemed especially strong, and my vision was more acute than usual. I sat down on a set of concrete outdoor steps to take in the day. There was a small tree next to me, covered with small, just-opening flower buds. The tree, less than a foot away from me, captured my attention. I studied the beautiful buds, the gray bark, and the shape of the little tree. I saw more than usual. I was looking out at the tree from a very special state of mind, fully present, especially open. I let the tree go and brought my attention to my state of mind. I felt a clarity along with the energetic peacefulness. The moment stayed with me for the rest of my life—a moment of knowing.

As time went by, Maxima attracted more people. Soon Mark was surrounded by forty adoring students. His sense of himself began to inflate. Maxima became a cult of personality more than a group of people sincerely working to be more aware.

After I had lived in the teaching house for about a year, we held a New Year's Eve party. A small moment told me my days with Maxima were over. The party was ending, and everyone was leaving. Mark helped a woman student with her coat. While I was watching, I saw him leave his hands on her shoulders a little too long. In those few seconds, I knew they were having an affair.

Gurdjieff and Buddhism

The next day, Mark told us his wife, my dear friend Rebecca, had left with her daughter. He said she had gone away to seek enlightenment. I doubted that "seeking her enlightenment" was the real explanation for Rebecca's departure.

Within a few days, she telephoned me and confirmed my thoughts. She had discovered his affair, and she had left him. We met secretly, and our friendship deepened as we both struggled with Mark's perfidy and the changes it necessitated in our lives. Mark had set himself up as an example of an enlightened being. Then, after we had embraced him as a teacher, he proved himself to be nothing of the sort.

I cared deeply for many of my friends who were Maxima members, I didn't want to hurt the group. I made a plan that would do the least damage and spent three months—from that New Year's Eve party—until April first, preparing to leave. I shared my thoughts with no one. Leaving felt like turning my back on my friends. I didn't want anyone else to have to go through the disappointment that I was feeling. I had wasted so much time with a false teacher.

On April first, I announced I was leaving and moved out the same day. Later, I learned that Mark had made deprecating remarks about me at his next Sunday talk. He had told the group to shun me. He used that actual word! This confirmed my view of him as a false teacher. In spite of his instructions, several of my close friends from Maxima called me and stayed in touch. They were having their own doubts.

The group fell apart within a few months. Mark's problems became more and more obvious to everyone. Most of the members left Maxima.

I moved to a nearby apartment building. I knew about the building because I had been seeing an acupuncturist named John Prester who lived and practiced there. Acupuncture was again helping me to recover from a difficult situation. I found an apartment downstairs, and we became good friends. Counseling went along with his acupuncture treatments, and he encouraged me to talk about and explore how I felt about the loss of my spiritual path and my teacher.

One day, he told me he was starting a Buddhist meditation group in his apartment. When he was younger, in the late 1960s and the 1970s, he had traveled in Asia to study Buddhism. He had been friends with the founders of American Buddhism, Joseph Goldstein and Jack Kornfield, along with other young American seekers, like Ram Dass and Timothy Leary. Together, they studied with the dozen or so Asian Buddhist masters of the time: Ajahn Chah in Thailand, U Pandita in Burma, the Sixteenth Karmapa in Nepal, and Goenka in India.

I attended John's newly forming Buddhist meditation group. I took the elevator up one flight. The door was open, and a small group sat in a circle on the floor in his living room. As I stepped into the apartment, I fell face forward on the floor just inside the door. As the shock of falling wore off, I got up slowly and moved to sit in the circle with the others. Somehow the fall didn't hurt me, almost as if it had happened symbolically, marking this new and important moment in my life.

There was a funny feeling in my heart and stomach. I remembered the moment of knowing on the kindergarten playground so many years ago. I remembered how Marilyn Cloud had made me cry, and that in response, I had made a vow to be kind. Now, this was another moment of knowing, here in this circle of Buddhist meditators.

I joined the meditation group and rediscovered mindfulness in a new setting. John was not only a wonderful acupuncturist, but he was also a good meditation teacher. He taught me beginning practices that have lasted my whole life: mindfulness of the body and mindfulness of breathing. Each week, I looked forward to our group.

Buddhism differs profoundly from the Gurdjieff work. The main difference is Buddhism emphasizes opening the heart and being kind. In the Gurdjieff work, we are taught that anyone who is not practicing self-remembering is "food for worms." Despite all the other good teachings, this phrase sums up a callous and dismissive side of Gurdjieff's teachings.

I understood that mindfulness without kindness is not mindfulness at all. It's merely attention, which is not the same. Think of a cat burglar who is robbing a home in the night. He works to be alert and attentive to everything that is going on—everything except his harmful intentions and dishonesty. One can be attentive but not mindful. True mindfulness understands the beauty and connectedness of all things, and it honors that with gentleness and care.

As I was discovering Buddhism in Philadelphia, Stuart was discovering Buddhism out West. We were even exploring the same branch of Buddhism, Theravada Buddhism, Vipassana, also known as Insight Meditation. Stu came back East, and we went on a ten-day silent retreat together in West Virginia. We sat with the Buddhist monk, Bhante Gunaratana, and he was a wonderful teacher.

That experience sealed our relationship, and soon after, I moved to be with Stuart. We lived near a teacher Stu knew, John Travis. John was, and remains, very much the teacher of my heart.

Thirty years later, Stu and I are both still active Buddhist practitioners, still studying with John, still enjoying a life of being present and working to be kind—kind to one another, kind to ourselves, kind to all beings.

I was only a short drive from Renaissance Winery, the

center of the Gurdjieff group at the Fellowship of Friends in Marysville, CA. I went to visit and signed up for an orientation series, which met once a week for a few weeks. I walked around the property and spoke with people.

Mark had told everyone at Maxima that his teacher had sent him to Philadelphia to start a Fourth Way group. However, the winery center workers told me Mark had been expelled from the Fellowship of Friends because he had physically mistreated the woman who was his partner. I might have become alienated from all spiritual practices at that point, but I had moved on to the kinder and more gentle practice of Buddhism. This helped me to leave the falseness of Maxima behind.

Chartres
Cathedral

I n the late 1980s, while I was still in the Gurdjieff group in Philadelphia, I went to France with a friend who was also in the group. The purpose of our trip was to visit Chartres Cathedral, located about fifty miles from Paris. My travel companion was a lawyer and had studied dance for many years. She was good company, especially because we were both very interested in Chartres.

Formally named The Cathedral of Our Lady of Chartres, the building was constructed around the year 1200. Before then, the site had hosted at least five other cathedrals, starting in around 400 when Christianity first came to France. It's felt locally that there was something very special about the site of Chartres, something that called for a spiritual center.

Chartres is one of the most beautiful and historic cathedrals in all of Europe, a masterpiece of High Gothic architecture. There are over 150 stained glass windows, many of soaring height. The building has three great facades, each adorned with dozens of stone figures representing biblical stories and themes. Its spire is almost four hundred feet high, quite an architectural feat for the times.

Moments of Knowing

In the 1200s, people with building skills sought out the sites in Europe where cathedrals were being built. The church granted indulgences—forgiveness of sins—to anyone who helped in the building of a cathedral. Since cathedrals took centuries to build, these were lifetime jobs. They were also exciting jobs, with generous budgets. The cathedrals were meant to be lavish, demonstrating the community's enthusiasm to reflect the glory of God.

Hundreds of workers gathered together in Chartres. There were simple laborers, as well as highly skilled workers, such as masons, stonecutters, and sculptors. Stained glass skills were highly valued as large windows became an important part of cathedral design. Word would spread, and hopeful workers traveled across the country.

Not only was Chartres Cathedral almost four hundred feet high, but it sat atop a high hill. As my friend and I traveled in our rental car from Paris, we saw the cathedral as a recognizable shape on the horizon. I imagined the workers in the Middle Ages traveling along this same route from Paris, perhaps in a horse-drawn wagon carrying several artisans and their masonry or stonecutting tools. How inspiring it must have been for them to see the beginnings of the cathedral beckoning them to a new life.

The first thing I did when we arrived in Chartres was to walk around the building, starting at the great West Facade. From there, I continued down the little side street until I stood in front of the South entryway. This doorway was surrounded by life-size sculptures. The figure of Christ stood in the middle on the column between two enormous wooden doors. Six of his twelve disciples stood to the right of the doors and the other six to the left.

Like these disciples, there were sculptures of biblical characters along the outside of the church. Their faces were so life-like, each so real-looking and unique. I imagined that the sculptors had been inspired by the faces of their fellow workers. Hundreds of stone figures graced the building. I felt surrounded by the presence of these workers from more than a thousand years ago.

The north side of the church was a lush green park, and there were fewer decorations. It was a place to stop and take a breath.

Finally, I was back at the West Facade. I gazed at the three great arched doorways in the center entry with their heavy wooden portals. Above was the beautiful rose window. Finally, I had to lean back to see the two tall towers on either side.

My friend and I had come to Chartres with a primary goal. We wanted to walk the labyrinth. For us it would be meditation, a walk that symbolized walking the spiritual path of life. We would do everything we could to stay mindful and keep our hearts and minds open as we walked. I had looked forward to this moment, and I knew I would cherish the experience. I hoped it would help me to leave behind the quotidian concerns that take up so much of each day, and instead to spend more time in my higher mind, aware of my life and more conscious of each situation.

Cultures in all times and places had their labyrinths: Native American labyrinths; Egyptian pyramid labyrinths; Greek myth labyrinths; and ancient Chinese cave labyrinths. Every labyrinth had its own shape, size, and pathways. The online worldwide Labyrinth Locator lists five thousand labyrinths in eighty countries.

A labyrinth differs from a maze. A maze is made up of branching paths and directions, with multiple possible entrances and exits. When you walk a maze, you can go round and round, sometimes retracing steps you have already taken. It's meant to be confusing. A labyrinth has one and only one entrance. That entrance leads along one and only one path. The path never branches, and there is never a decision to be made.

Originally many of the medieval European cathedrals had labyrinths like Chartres, but most of them were destroyed, with Chartres one of the few remaining. The labyrinth at Chartres was built in the nave of the church, the main central part of the church where people came to worship.

It's a circular design, forty-two feet in diameter. The pathways are outlined by strips of midnight-blue marble. Under normal circumstances, it takes about half an hour to walk. There are 270 stones to walk across, representing the number of days in the nine months of human gestation.

There are eleven concentric circles, weaving in and out. At the center is a beautiful rose pattern of stones. The outer circles represent our outer life in the physical world. The inner circle represents our deepest spirituality. Walking the labyrinth is a pilgrimage, a symbolic life's journey, slowly and carefully done with mindfulness, every step its own moment. Labyrinths around the world have been based on the design of the Chartres labyrinth.

As my friend and I entered the nave, we were shocked to see that the labyrinth was completely covered with dozens of small, folding, wooden chairs. We both suspected that the church had set up the chairs to discourage labyrinth walkers. I assumed the officials of the church saw the labyrinth as a somewhat pagan symbol that encouraged pagan activities, certainly not anything essentially Catholic. I thought the chairs were their way of communicating this attitude. I felt great disappointment as I thought how the chairs would prevent us from walking the labyrinth, despite our having crossed an ocean to do so.

Chartres Cathedral

But I had underestimated my travel companion. I will always be grateful to her for what she did next. She very deliberately moved herself to the entry point. She stood there for a moment, taking a deep breath of beginning. Then, moving like a dancer, she reached down in front of herself and picked up the lightweight chair that was blocking her way. She put one hand on each side of the chair, and then she swung the entire chair into the air to her side. She took a step forward, and then swung the chair back down behind her and set it on the floor. Step one had been taken. She picked up the next chair in front of her.

I watched her dancer-trained movements for a minute before realizing I could do the same thing. I walked up to the labyrinth entrance and reached down for my first chair. It worked. I reached for the second chair. I made every effort to be fully present to every movement and to the labyrinth, to the stones and the surrounding cathedral. I was engaged.

Even though there were no decisions to be made, even though the path was always right before me, I found the labyrinth challenging. I was concerned. Perhaps I had accidentally stepped over a line in error, not following a pathway correctly. I imagined ending up back at the beginning instead of in the beautiful center. Looking back now, these concerns remind me of my concerns about life itself.

I am not always sure of the paths I have taken. I hope I have stayed true and not stepped over the lines of life.

It was hours before we reached the center. But the moment when I picked up my last chair, the moment when I took my first step into the center rose, that is a moment I will always remember. A moment of knowing.

I stood still. There was a special peace and completeness about all things. After a bit, I took in my surroundings. I looked up into the vaulted ceiling that soared more than one hundred feet above. The rose window and the other stained-glass windows splashed jewel-like colors all around, beautiful geometry everywhere in delicately carved stone tracery. The surroundings were a perfect match for a perfect moment.

Computer
Programming

In the mid-to-late 1970s, I was around thirty-five years old. I lived in a large brick building on a narrow side street in Philadelphia. The building had been a three-story warehouse, but an older artist, Mario Zubari, had bought the building and renovated it to be his studio space. Mario was a successful artist. He designed tiles and composed tile walls and spaces for many clients. He made enough money practicing his art to live well. His work was beautiful. Mario lived on the third floor, and he rented his second floor to me.

The second floor was divided in half. The front half was a thirty-foot-square finished living space with twenty-foot ceilings and several fifteen-foot-high windows. It was a beautiful space. The view out the windows was of local alleyways, but the alleys supported tall Ailanthus trees and filled my windows with green. The basic kitchen and bathroom fitted nicely into one corner of the space—just a few counters and the necessary fixtures. A half-height fridge was tucked under a kitchen counter.

This large space had a continuous loft about twelve feet high, all the way around the room, easily accessible by a comfortable staircase in one corner. No ladders were needed. The loft area was ideal for sleeping and storage. In one corner of the loft, over the kitchen-bathroom area, was an enormous white clawfoot bathtub that you could see from anywhere in the loft. A bathtub in plain view was kind of an interior design statement of freedoms unknown to previous generations. It seemed to ask why we shouldn't all be relaxed while a naked person took a bath in front of whomever was around.

A "fireplace" hung in the middle of the room and warmed everything. It was a five-foot-high steel box with a big door to throw in wood or anything else that would burn. Metal chimney pipes connected the box to the outdoors. This large woodstove kept the entire loft both warm and cozy. Mario was an inspired builder.

The place had more than its share of cockroaches that were typical in most large cities. I had read that Jackie Onassis had cockroaches in her New York apartment, which made me feel better, knowing I shared the problem with the wealthy and famous.

The back half of the building's second floor was not renovated. It was still an old warehouse space, roughly subdivided into smaller spaces that lent themselves to being artwork areas. One area I set up for painting, with my easel and several large tables for paints, brushes, and bottles. I had lots of room to make large canvases. If I wanted to, I could put a canvas on the floor and throw paint just like Jackson Pollock. This wasn't particularly my way of painting, but I tried it a few times. It was fun, but my results were not inspiring.

I had read about Pollock throwing paint at the canvas and didn't expect to like his work. The prints in books were not interesting. But unexpectedly, when I went to New York's Museum of Modern Art and saw his original work, spreading enormously ten feet across a wall, I found it beautiful and inspiring. He was doing more than just "throwing" paint. Or perhaps he was demonstrating that the uncontrolled accident had its own special beauty.

My boyfriend at that time was George Kotmayer. Everyone called him Georgie K. He was an electronic musician and an all-around tech guy. I always enjoyed his company. He was so smart as to be irresistible. There was never a shortage of conversation and investigation between us. Georgie came over often, and I invited him to set up part of my back area as a studio for his music.

In between creating masterpieces on canvas, I hung around to see what Georgie was doing. His studio area was a mystery of small music machines that he mostly made himself. He had a homemade synthesizer that put out electronic music that was unlike acoustic music of the past. The room would fill with sheets of electronic sounds, repeating endlessly, with small changes every so often, gradually becoming something else, which sometimes sounded like pure electricity or a piano or a human voice mixed in. I enjoyed listening to these new sounds.

I begged Georgie to show me how to play electronic music. He explained what each little box of circuits and tubes did and what its contribution was to the overall sound. He had built a sequencer—whatever that was—and a drum box that could produce a serious beat. Reverb pedals went under my feet. The lead singer, whom Georgie called "Theresa 80," had previously been a normal TRS-80 computer from Radio Shack. Once Georgie was done teaching her to sing, Theresa had turned into a green plastic Z-80 motherboard covered in chips and other incomprehensible hardware. There was no screen, keyboard, mouse, or anything civilized. The personal computer had only existed for about five years. But Georgie was practically living in the future.

He taught me just enough so that I could sit in the middle

of the equipment, push buttons, turn dials, and see what happened. Soon I was holding down three buttons at once and turning dials left and right to create my own diaphanous streams of abstract sound, winding through the octaves, slowly changing from one sound to another. I was working in a new art form. The buttons and dials were my new paints.

Georgie and his friends had a performing electronic music band called Heavenside Layer. The name was a takeoff on "Heaviside Layer," a part of the earth's atmosphere. His group played at local bars and clubs, and even did a concert at the Theater of the Living Arts, a local spot that could seat 1,000 people. Georgie's good friend Ron Thomas was part of the band. Ron had taken Georgie to play with his music teacher at the University of Pennsylvania, Karlheinz Stockhausen. Stockhausen liked what he heard, and Georgie, Ron, and Karlheinz had performed together at Lincoln Center in Manhattan. Georgie was good at music.

With no screen, keyboard, or mouse, it was not easy to communicate with Theresa 80. Somehow Georgie got a used paper tape reader and lugged it up into his music studio at my place. This smooth silver metal device stood taller than me. Like everything in Georgie's area, it had a lot of small red lights that went on and off. It could spit out or take in long, narrow streams of paper that had holes punched all over, apparently in meaningful patterns. Georgie figured out how to communicate with Theresa 80 by punching holes in the paper and feeding them into this device. I had no idea how he punched the holes or what they meant. But Georgie knew what he was doing.

I was rapt. Only a few times in my life have I been so instantly and magnetically drawn to a configuration of things: watercolor painting, meditation, and walking in the woods.

How varied are the activities that transport us.

Georgie taught me how computers worked. He explained

the basic principle: electricity had only two states, on and off. It was all that was needed to do anything. By detecting the difference between these two states, computers do everything: mathematics; language; music; running Fortune 500 companies; guiding satellites around the planet; sending spaceships to other planets; performing robotic surgery; and all the way up to serving as a model of the human brain and of our thought processes.

I always liked to start with the basics, so Georgie showed me how to count in binary. He explained what we do when we do regular counting with decimal numbers. I had never analyzed the process the way he did, so it was impressive to hear him take apart something I had done since first grade without really understanding what I was doing. Georgie explained how counting worked in decimal, then showed me how to count in binary and octal. I was amazed.

He made me write down all the binary numbers from 0 to 256. He checked my work and declared I had everything right. It's more than forty years later, but I can still feel the good feeling when I got to 256.

I was completely and passionately in love with everything about binary numbers and computers. Within a month, I had shifted focus. My paints were drying up, and my canvases lay askew in my studio. I took all my savings and enrolled in a three-month computer tech training program. My first day at computer school was a moment of knowing. I could see that the whole human race was going to love these machines and take them on a long ride down new pathways of understanding. There would be music, art, intelligence, and many different kinds of communication. I was thrilled that I was going to be part of making it all happen.

The Computer
Learning Center

My three-month training started in 1980. I was lucky because the Computer Learning Center, where I enrolled, was a good school. It was part of a nation-wide chain of for-profit technical schools that taught computer programming. It wasn't one of the many rip-off schools prolifer-ating at the time. Computer Learning Center was well run, and the curriculum was well thought out. There were small classes, great teachers, and lots of great computer equipment to learn about and use.

The school had its own IBM System/360, a state-of-the-art, mainframe computer. Mainframes had been around since the 1950s, and by the 1970s, every large business in the United States had its own mainframe, usually the same model as ours. The IBM/360 was a huge box that took up an entire room. It sported a $250,000 price tag. This was computer royalty, and that's how we treated it.

Our computer was housed in its own glass room. We gazed admiringly through the pale-green glass, but no student was ever allowed to enter. I contemplated the flashing red lights on every box and panel. A pair of twenty-four-inch diameter

The Computer Learning Center

tape drives spun around, delivering data. They were the "hard drives" of the day. It was a marvel.

The school required that we take three four-week courses, starting with Introduction to Computer Programming. This course taught us how computers worked, what all the hardware was, the history of how computers came to be, and some things about early software. Our first project, I am proud to say, was the traditional first project in every computer programming course. We wrote a program to print out the words, "Hello, World."

Years later I was a teaching assistant in computer programming courses at the University of Pennsylvania. I started every programming class with that same Hello World program. The Hello World program illustrated that a new being had joined the world and was politely saying, "Hello" before doing all the other things it could do.

———

Our second course at Computer Learning Center was learning to write code in COBOL, a popular computer language, common for use in business. COBOL tried to be friendly. The language was like English, so that it could be read like regular sentences. The language had commands like "Print report," or "Add 1 to 2."

Forty years later, COBOL is still a popular language for business programming.

With COBOL, it seemed like I could do anything that had ever been done with pen and paper. I wrote paychecks, printed out reports, set up an address book, and created labels. Of course, these everyday office projects were not the point. For me, the point was the enjoyable brainwork of analyzing how a job was done, step-by-step in tiny increments. The product of that analysis was called an "algorithm." It described, in English, each step in the procedure for solving a specific problem. Once I had an algorithm, I could convert each step into a command in a programming language, like COBOL. Those commands would tell the computer what to do.

Computer Learning Center's third and final course was Assembly Language, a much more difficult language. Every computer had its own assembly language, which arises out of whatever the computer can do internally, such as add, subtract, multiply, divide, etc.

Communication with the big computer was by punched cards, a state-of-the-art medium at the time, but with a long history. Punched cards came from the old textile industry. They were invented in the early 1700s in France for use in weaving, specifically for programming looms to create specialty fabrics.

A French textile engineer named Jacquard created a loom that could read punched cards. When there was a hole in the card, a mechanism reached through the hole and picked up a thread. If there wasn't a hole, the thread was left alone. Endlessly beautiful fabrics could be created with this simple idea.

Today, luxurious Jacquard silks can be bought. Looms still work the same way, albeit not with punched cards.

Computers picked up where the textile industry left off. Lots of computer technology came from textiles, and the language of computers reflected this.

For example, programs have loops just like yarn does. Printers have spools. If you follow my thread . . .

At about the same time Jacquard worked in Lyon, France, a British math student named Charles Babbage worked in Cambridge. Babbage won an award for his work creating a new calculating machine. It had 25,000 parts and was funded by a government grant. Babbage used Jacquard's punched cards to program his machine. Hole or no hole? A simple way to count in binary. If there was a hole, turn the electricity off. If there was not a hole, let the electricity flow. As I had learned in my early binary counting days, everything needed was right there with the on and off.

Babbage was forward-thinking. For many years he had been a mentor and friend to the Countess Ada Lovelace. He inspired her to study mathematics at Cambridge. Both Babbage and the countess were from privileged and wealthy families. She was the daughter of the poet, Lord Byron, but it was not her relationship to the poet that earned her place in history. It was her keen mind and passion for programming. When Babbage showed Lovelace his new computer, she became the first computer programmer. She saw the potential of the computer; she even spoke of its composing music one day.

In 1830, it was difficult to manufacture the needed parts for Babbage's computers. For that reason, his most advanced computer, the Analytical Engine, wasn't built until the twenty-first century. It was the first computer. Although Babbage was gone, the machine worked exactly as he said it would.

There is a portrait of Babbage, woven in silk by Jacquard on his loom. He gave the portrait to Babbage as a present. The computer grew in part from the art of Jacquard. His loom could put together colors, patterns, and designs of the greatest complexity. There were no computer graphics yet, but one could imagine they were coming soon.

In 1977, the US Department of Defense created a computer language called Ada. The new language replaced the 450 different computer languages the department had been using before that time and was an honor to Ada Lovelace.

There I was in the late 1970s with some great enthusiasm

for computers and even a bit of knowledge. I had my decks of punched cards and my much-admired IBM mainframe behind glass. I was embarking on an adventure that would sustain my interest and imagination for the rest of my life.

All this came to me because of the imagination and creativity of men and women over a two-hundred-year period. I was grounded in the past, in the history of what I was doing. I prepared for my future on this new journey. I loved every minute of my time at the Computer Learning Center. My work, like all computer science work must be, was as exact and perfect as I could make it.

When I completed the course, the school offered me a job as an instructor. I taught all their classes for a time but ended up specializing in assembly language, preferring it because it reflected how the machine worked. They say that assembly language is "close to the metal."

Throughout my life I could always passionately teach whatever I was passionately doing. My job at the Computer Learning Center was my first job in this new area. Jobs in the computer field were appearing, and I waited on the doorstep.

Programming
Jobs

In 1980, once I completed my studies at the Computer Learning Center, I was in a great position, ready to enter the emerging computer industry with a good grasp and a love of programming.

I found a job with the Philadelphia Fire Department, programming their 911 emergency ambulance dispatch system. I worked in the basement of Philadelphia's Fire Department headquarters. My little office was off the big room where all the fire emergency calls came in, as well as the emergency medical 911 calls. Our computer handled the medical calls. A half dozen or so operators manned our phones. My computer displayed the screens that helped the operators answer the calls and dispatch the ambulances.

When a call came in, the operator entered the address where the medical emergency was taking place. The computer knew where every ambulance was at all times, and it could figure out which ambulance was closest to the emergency. Operators could dispatch the closest ambulance within seconds.

Our emergency computer was smart. When ambulances were not working, the vehicles would wait for the next call. Since the system kept records of past emergencies, it could predict where the next one was statistically likely to occur. Ambulances waited as close as possible to this probable next place. With a heart attack, an ambulance had only four minutes to arrive at the scene for the best hope of saving the person. Minutes mattered. Lives were saved by ones and zeroes.

My second computer programming job was for Blue Cross. I hated it. I worked in a glass cubicle and was forced to write boring COBOL programs about insurance. I barely managed to stay the one year required so as not to "ruin my resume." In those days, when working with computers, if someone left a job before a year was out, it was seen as a failure. When my year-long sentence was up, I was happy to move on.

Jobs were everywhere, and for a long time I was able to change jobs each year and enjoy large salary increases. After ten years, I was making more money than I could spend. My bank balance was higher than ever. I was used to living on a hippie budget, and not used to having money in the bank.

I loved the work. And I still do. Even today, I get caught up with the process of writing a program. What is it about programming that is so compelling for me? I believe it is a truly creative activity. I am the architect, the one who names everything, the one who knows where everything is kept and how to get to it. This is my city, and it quickly becomes my world.

My worlds have a consistency—I always create the same structures in the same way, even for very different applications. I have a set of small programming techniques that I feel confident about. I always program in a simple yet overstated way so that everything is easy to understand. Easy for me to understand and also for any future maintenance programmer who may have to work with my code after I have moved on. Sometimes, things need to be changed years later, and I wanted that future programmer to easily understand the code.

Programming Jobs

Many programmers enjoy writing code that is fast, uses the fewest possible commands, and is flashy and impressive. It's almost like there is a "stylish" way to write code. But that kind of code is always harder to understand later. So, I never do that. I work hard to write simple and easy-to-read code. Sometimes it may be more plodding, but it is always as easy to follow as can be.

The programming worlds that I create become comfortable for me. Let's create paychecks. Let's sign up for a course and keep track of everyone who signs up, how much they paid, and how much they still owe. Let's get everyone's email, phone, address, etc. Instead of Georgie K.'s paper tape machine, I now have a database stored in the cloud. New computer languages can reach up to the cloud and pull down whatever they need without a single punched hole.

My next job was the best job of all. I worked for a little company called ROCAPPI: Research on Computer Applications for the Printing and Publishing Industries. ROCAPPI invented using computers to typeset and publish books. Our big project during my time with them was computerizing the book, *Who's Who in America*.

Previously, we had set physical type and printed *Who's Who* on paper. But the time had come. We needed to move everything onto the computer. Future editions of *Who's Who in America* could be updated on the computer by clerical staff. Each year's edition could be printed directly from the computer. No more physical typesetting.

To computerize *Who's Who in America*, we followed a process that our team designed together. The first step was for the secretaries at ROCAPPI to type out the entire book using word processors. Early word processors were rapidly coming into common use, and they made this part of the job much easier.

Moments of Knowing

Once the secretaries were done, the book existed as a set of computer text files, like Microsoft Word documents, with sentences, pages, etc.

As programmers, our big project was to get the computer to read these text files and then move all the information they contained into a database. Our database would have one record for each person in *Who's Who*. For each person, we would have specific columns of information: first name, last name, date of birth, place of birth, parents, employer, awards, etc.

We were a tight-knit team of five programmers. We worked together closely, always helping one another. I was thirty-six years old, and the others in the group were in their thirties as well. Since I was the newest to programming and also the only woman in the group, some of the guys were like older brothers to me. They helped me along and gave me good ideas for the best ways to write the code I was responsible for.

We were all devoted to our boss, Rick, mostly because he was the smartest and funniest guy in the room. He had his own tiny office with just enough room for him behind the desk and one or two of us on the other side. We had to walk by his office to get to our cubicles. But he never watched us or worried about our commitment to the job. He trusted us because he knew we cared as much about doing good work as he did.

Every day, Rick wore maroon polyester pants that were too short and shirts with every button straining at its buttonhole. His lack of attention to his appearance didn't bother me. Rick taught me more about computers than anyone else. I adored Rick for the way he trusted us, his kindness as he shared his brilliant ideas, and his leadership.

Our master program had to read the text entry for one person in *Who's Who*. Then we could run that program over and over for each person in the book. The program had to be smart enough to extract the specific information we needed about each person. This was challenging because the text we had, from old editions of *Who's Who*, was free-ranging text that had no specific format or standardized keywords. We solved the problem by searching the old text for a variety of keywords that might occur, such as "date of birth," or "born." After eight months of programming, the entire volume of *Who's Who* was on a large tape reel on our mainframe in the form of a database—a row for each person and columns for each piece of data.

The last part of our programming project was to write programs that could read this new database and turn it back into a friendly and readable volume of *Who's Who*. It had to look and feel like all the volumes of *Who's Who* that had been published before, since 1898. This, too, was a success.

Finally, we had to write maintenance programs to allow changes to the content. Office personnel at the *Who's Who* company would now be able to update a person's information. In addition, they could enter a new person or even delete someone, although it is hard to imagine that ever being needed. Once famous, always famous!

To work on one of my programs at ROCAPPI, I sat at my desk in our small programming department. My computer terminal was connected to ROCAPPI's five-ton mainframe computer. I would enter some new code and run my program. Then I waited until the next morning to see my printed output with any error messages. Each morning, I walked down to the big, air-conditioned printer room and retrieve yesterday's report on green-and-white striped computer paper. There was no Internet yet, so programs produced paper results. There were no results on the screen. Turnaround time was twenty-four hours.

It's remarkable how much easier it is to test my programs today, forty years later. Now, when I write a program, I go to

Moments of Knowing

Starbucks for a cup of coffee and park my two-pound laptop at one of their tables. I change a few lines of code, upload my file to the Internet, and run it just like my end users will do. A few moments later, if it works, I'm done. If there are problems, I change the code to fix the problem, then upload and run it again. I repeat this sequence until everything is perfect. My turnaround time for each change is maybe two minutes, as opposed to twenty-four hours.

One day at ROCAPPI, I wrote a program for a client that contained an accidental bug. The client was a textbook publishing company named Baker & Taylor in Reno, Nevada. I was creating a sales report for them. At the top of each page, there were headings such as any report might have, the company name "Baker & Taylor," the report title, a page number over in the upper right corner, and a date on the left. It was supposed to be about a twenty-page report.

I accidentally left off a period at the end of a line of code. The code that I wrote without the period had far-reaching consequences. Because of my leaving off the period, the computer didn't know when to stop. When I came in the next morning and went down to the printer room to get my latest twenty-page report with my latest changes, the printer room guy said to me, "Your report is over there in those fourteen boxes."

Presumably, some reports actually needed fourteen boxes to be complete, so the printer room guy was not concerned, considering it an ordinary report. He had no way of knowing I was expecting only twenty pages, not 14,000.

I opened the first box and looked at my report. Each sheet of green-and-white striped paper had nothing on it but headings without any actual information—just fourteen boxes of headings. Page numbers went right up into the thousands. I had wasted fourteen boxes of paper. I panicked.

"Thanks so much," I said. "I'll take two boxes now and come back for more in a minute." I wanted to avoid running into anyone who might wonder what I was doing, so I took a little-traveled hallway out to my car and dumped the boxes in the trunk and back seat. Seven more trips and the evidence was gone. No one ever found out. But I can feel the memory of my panic just thinking about it.

Back to School Makes All "the Difference"

My father went to Georgia Tech and graduated with a degree in electrical engineering. In 1939, he was one of the first three Jewish boys to be admitted to this southern school. They were assigned to one another as dorm roommates. My father's two roommates became my "uncles." Uncle Bob and Uncle Al took an interest in me for the rest of their lives.

In spite of how much I was enjoying my new computer career, my father was not happy about my trade school credentials from the Computer Learning Center.

"You deserve better," he said.

He offered to send me back to school for a master's degree in computer science, all expenses paid.

I started taking night classes at the University of Pennsylvania, an Ivy League school in Philadlephia. Because I had been an undergraduate English major, there were quite a few undergrad courses I needed to take before I could enter a graduate computer science program, mostly math and computer science prerequisites. I was motivated, and I got perfect

Back to School Makes All "the Difference"

A's. After a year, I applied to the graduate program and was accepted.

When my dad found out I had gotten into an Ivy League school, he was ecstatic. As a first-generation college graduate and the son of immigrants from Europe with no higher education, he was overly impressed by Ivy League credentials. I am probably the same way. I love it that my dentist went to Harvard. Also, I think it's dumb that I care about this. But I do.

My dad did well in business. As a result, he served on the boards of several electronics companies. He bought a lot of stock in an engineering company he worked with, at about 5 cents a share. Over twenty years, he watched that stock climb to $75 a share. From then on, he had no financial worries. I knew he would have no trouble paying my $50,000 a year tuition at Penn, thanks to his smart investing.

I look back now and realize that I figured out a useful back door to acceptance by an Ivy League school.

Take night courses in general studies. Most schools will admit anyone into general studies, so it's easy to start out that way. Get perfect As in every course taken. Look up the prerequisites for the degree desired. In the College of General Studies, take those prerequisites if possible. Finally, apply for the degree program. They will look at the straight As in the prerequisite programs for the degree, and you may very well be accepted.

Graduate school took my understanding of computers to a new level. My professors were not really interested in the type of work I had been doing writing programs to produce reports. Not even the 911 dispatch system impressed them. They were interested in how the computer is an extension of our brain, how it is evolving into a model of our brain. They were exploring how the design of brain systems, such as neural networks, could be templates for computer design, and how computers would ultimately allow us to better understand ourselves and our own intelligence and how it works.

Two years later in 1981, Ivy League degree in hand, I was applying for a different kind of job. My first application was to Microsoft. They flew me to Redmond, Washington. I drove my rental car through endless drizzles of rain to the large Microsoft campus.

They were thorough, assigning fourteen different people to interview me over three days. I was in my forties now, and my interviewers were mostly in their twenties and loved their jobs. But two of the interviewers were my own age, and they both said the same thing to me.

"Don't take this job. You will hate it here." They explained to me that Microsoft was like an Ivy League school extension, mostly twenty-year-old kids just out of prestigious schools, highly competitive, and in the bar drinking beer whenever they were not at work.

Microsoft offered me a job. I thought about the rain and about the twenty-somethings and the beer, and I turned it down. Today I sometimes regret not having been at Microsoft as they grew and dominated the software markets. I would have made a lot of money if I had gotten in early. But I knew it hadn't been right for me. Another important factor was that I didn't want to move to a new place where I didn't know any-one. I had friends in Philadelphia, and it would be too hard to give them up.

My other big interview was with IBM. They had a contract with the Federal Aviation Administration to write a new Air Traffic Control System for the entire United States. It looked like a good project, but I would have had to move to Washing-ton, DC. Just as with the Microsoft job, I wasn't ready to move and leave my good friends in Philadelphia.

Back to School Makes All "the Difference"

It's a good thing I didn't take the IBM job because the project was a spectacular failure. It was the first in a series of failures to rewrite the Air Traffic Control System. Many decades have passed, and billions of dollars have been spent, but a fully functional Air Traffic Control computer system has never been achieved.

Today's Air Traffic Control relies as little as possible on automation, and that's why it works so well.

Finally, I took a job with a Fortune 500 company, Saatchi & Saatchi. They had many businesses under their worldwide umbrella, and this business was a Philadelphia management consulting company. There were two hundred partners, all Wharton graduates. Wharton was the business school of the University of Pennsylvania, and my degree from the same school sealed the deal.

The management consulting firm that I worked for is still the world leader in defining appropriate salaries, as in "who should make how much money." My company was the leader in salary consulting all over the world for huge companies with offices in multiple countries and for thousands of different job titles.

The company had resisted computers, all the partners having been at Wharton before computers became common. In 1981, they realized they needed to move their expertise onto a computerized platform. Toward that end, they hired people like me. I could feel that nobody at the firm quite trusted us or our education. These Wharton grads looked at us computer people like we were low-level technicians. It was just the culture of the place, and I tried not to take it personally.

There were three of us hired as managers. We collaborated on creating a new programming department, hiring twenty-five C++ programmers. Over the next few years, these programmers built new systems to help the company do its work. The systems were very well done. Clients were presented with easy-to-understand computer graphics and charts that helped to explain the sometimes-complicated salary systems we designed. The partners worried that our programs would ultimately outstrip and replace them, which was probably true, but it was a long way off.

Huge international companies like AT&T hired us to set salaries for the entire company worldwide. We ensured telephone operators were not making more than telephone operator supervisors, even across national boundaries. It was complicated. But we had methods, and my group's job was to teach those methods to the computer.

About the time I joined the company, the partners came up with a new salary idea that made hiring us a "must" for every company in the world. The idea was, simply put, "Let's pay the CEO millions of dollars!" This was a popular idea, especially among CEOs. Before our new idea, CEOs made just a bit more than other top managers, maybe $100,000. Our idea was to pay CEOs a stratospheric amount more—millions of dollars more. We were hired by every CEO who could afford us. Our company became a world leader in salary consulting. CEOs around the world became wildly overpaid, as they still are to this day. This was great at the time, bringing in so much new business to my place of employment, but today, I look at these huge salaries somewhat askance.

My office overlooked Rittenhouse Square, Philadelphia's nicest downtown square, filled with trees and benches. My best friend Rebecca, whom I had known since our days at Maxima, came to work with me, and I enjoyed every day. I worked hard and was successful.

After twelve years at this job, I finally moved to California to be with Stu. It was the early 1990s by then and the Internet

Back to School Makes All "the Difference"

was getting started in a big way. I decided to build websites for a living. While there were many people with training in computers who could build a technically sound website, few of them knew anything about good color and design. I was lucky that my background combined art school and computer training. Many of my competitors were artistically talented graphic designers struggling to understand their new Apple computers, or they were technically savvy engineers who did not know anything about making a website attractive.

I started a small company, and over the next years, we built hundreds of websites for local and national businesses. I lived in California, in the Sierra Foothills with Stu, and life was good.

Georgia
Revisited

When I turned forty, I gave myself a birthday trip back to Augusta, Georgia, where I had lived with my mother and Art.

Over the past twenty-seven years, I had lost contact with my mother's family. They still lived in Augusta. My mother had two sisters, Doris and Bet, and two brothers, Freddy and Mitchell. I had also lost touch with my half-brother Artie Jr. and my half-sister Savannah. When our mother died, they had gone to live with their father, Art. I didn't actually "lose touch." I deliberately cut off all contact with my mother's family because I didn't want to remember being molested by Art.

After I moved away from Art, I didn't even allow myself to think that he might have moved on to molesting Savannah in place of me. Today, I realize that I suppressed those memories to survive, to let my new life heal me, and to let go of that past. However, I wish I had been older and wiser and able to let someone know that Savannah was in danger.

The last time I had seen or spoken to anyone in my mother's family was when she died. That was in 1956, when I was thirteen years old. When my father and I arrived at the church for the service, Aunt Bet was standing outside the church welcoming people. She looked so much like my mother that when many people first saw her, they were shocked and frightened, thinking it was my mother standing at her own funeral.

The strong pull drawing me back to Georgia was that I doubted some of my memories about what had happened there. I needed to verify that my childhood had actually happened as I remembered it. I needed to be with my aunts and see my cousins, to go where my young life had been lived and walk down the streets.

Maybe I was the problem. Maybe I imagined how mean Art was to me, maybe I dreamed up his abuse of me. I needed to verify that my memories were real. It was so unlike other people's more normal childhoods that I no longer quite believed some of it had happened.

I flew to Augusta, rented a car, and checked into a motel. I opened the phone book—there were phone books back then . . . one in every hotel room right next to the Bible. My mother's maiden name was Athearn. Everyone in her family was an Athearn. I just assumed there would be many in the phone book, especially since my mother had four siblings, who all had kids and most of them lived in Augusta. But to my surprise, there was not one Athearn in the book.

Most parents make their child memorize their address to tell the police if they get lost. I still knew our Augusta address by rote and could robotically recite it like any good four-year-old. "Twenty-Eight Royal Drive." I even remembered the name of the elementary school I had gone to, Joseph R. Lamar, and I was pretty sure I remembered how to walk home from school— most children can remember the walk they did every day.

I got the school address from the phone book, then asked a taxi driver to look at my free AAA map and show me how to get where I needed to go.

Moments of Knowing

I found the big brick entrance to my first school. There was the playground where I had experienced my very first moment of knowing, with Marilyn Cloud treating me badly, and my taking the vow to live for love. I was revisiting my history.

It was Saturday, so the school was deserted and no one else was around. I parked my rental car and began the walk home. Down the street, then a right turn onto a dirt path that went through the woods. After about five minutes in the woods, I came into a clearing with the white clapboard Baptist church where I had gone to Sunday School. I knew I was almost home because we lived just a block from the church.

No one in our family went to church but me. I knew Art and my mother were happy to get rid of me for a few hours every Sunday morning. I liked church. I liked singing, "Jesus Loves Me This I Know," with its chorus of "Yes, Jesus loves me" over and over. I always liked singing. For church, I got to wear a pretty dress and party shoes, an outfit always welcome in my world. I don't remember anything else about Sundays at church. Singing and fun clothes were my religion.

Forty-year-old me went up the church driveway. Standing at the church door, I turned around and looked up the hill. I could see our house at 28 Royal Drive. I walked up and stood in our yard. The house didn't look occupied. It was just a small wooden house of a nondescript color. I went around the house to look at the backyard. I remembered that Art had built a large swing set with kind of an A-frame construction. I remember being able to swing really high. The swing was gone now, and I was glad it wasn't there. After all the mean things he did, I didn't want to give Art credit for anything, even if it had been a good swing.

I walked back to the front yard, then across to the red clay ditch that ran all the way down Royal Drive in front of every house, separating the houses from the street. The ditch was only two- to three-feet deep, easy for kids to jump into. I remembered Patricia Williams, the older girl next door who sometimes was my babysitter when I was about five years old. I remembered she had told me the "facts of life" in that ditch. Patricia and I had run across the yard together and jumped into the ditch to be sure no one could hear us. We crouched down against the clay walls so that no one could see us.

Patricia had said in a whisper, "The man puts his thing inside the woman's thing." I don't think she knew much about what those "things" were, and neither did I. But my first introduction to the facts of life gave me a first glimpse into adulthood. Somehow, I knew this was important information.

I went up the steps onto the front porch, peeking through the windows. The house was empty with blank walls and linoleum floors. It looked run-down, with chipped paint and torn curtains in some of the windows, but it was still the same place. I remembered how scared I had been hiding behind the couch when the maid, Annie, had come that night and threw down all the things she had stolen.

By the time I was in third grade, the district had built a new school that was farther away, and I had to take a bus every morning. No more walking through the woods to Joseph R. Lamar Elementary. To get the bus I had to turn the corner and go up to the big street, Wheeler Road. That's where the bus stopped. We waited on our side of the street, and the Black kids waited across the street for their bus, which went in the opposite direction. This seemed completely normal, and I never questioned it.

Seeing the school, house, and church made me sure we had lived on Royal Drive. But I still had a lot of questions. I needed to meet some relatives.

Moments of Knowing

I remembered the address of Granny Mae, my mother's mother. I remember Granny Mae as a complete bitch. I don't think she ever said a nice word to me. I could do nothing right. I was happy just to keep away from her.

Granny Mae had a long-haired, white cat named Callie. One day when I was five, I had forgotten I wasn't supposed to pick Callie up because she would go crazy and scratch. I picked her up and got scratched all over my face, hands, and arms. Callie and Granny were two of a kind—if I didn't watch out, they would get me. Later in life I found out Granny was born the youngest of eight. She had seven older brothers, all of whom adored her. They called her, "Stormy." I knew why.

My only good memory of Granny was the patchwork quilts she made. Her quilts were on every bed in the house. We stayed over at her house often, and all the beds had Granny's quilts. In the morning, if I got all the way under the quilt, light shone through the pieces of fabric and enveloped me in a beautiful world of blocks of color, like stained glass only softer.

Quilts were made at quilting bees. When Granny had a quilting bee, people came through the front door into the living room, but then they had to put their backs up against the wall and sidle around the room to get into the rest of the house. The living room would be filled by a quilt in progress. It was strung on a frame that took up the whole room, with just enough room around the frame to surround it with small folding chairs. All of Granny's fellow quilters who came by to work on the project could take a seat and work on the project. This setup lasted for weeks until the quilt was done.

With the same rote memory of the child trained to recall her own address, the forty-year-old me could also recite Granny's address: "Twenty-One Nineteen Circular Drive."

Back to the hotel, back to the taxi driver, and the next

day, armed again with my free AAA map, I drove to Granny's. There it was, the same house, the same front yard, the same fields stretching away in the back, so many years later.

New people were living there, and once I explained who I was, they were friendly and helpful. They had bought the house from Granny Mae a few years earlier. She had been seventy-nine years old at the time. They said she was still climbing up on the roof to repair it herself.

I knew she had died recently because her will had been sent to me, not that I was mentioned in it. But in the will was an address for my half-brother, Artie, Jr. I wasn't ready to reach out to him, but I kept the document. Ten years later, when I was finally ready, that document was the key to finding him. In the will, Artie Jr.'s address was at West Point. He had followed in his military father's footsteps. A friend of a friend worked at the West Point offices and got me his address, which was the key that helped me find him, and then to find my sister Savannah.

The new owners at 2119 Circular Drive didn't know where any of my relatives might be. But they had an old phone book from five years earlier. We looked up Athearn, and there was my first cousin Warren Athearn. Warren was three years older than I. He was Uncle Freddy's kid, but he had grown up living with Granny Mae.

We were constant playmates when I moved to Georgia. Together, he and I built tunnels through the brown grass that was higher than we were, grass that covered the fields behind Granny Mae's house. We punched holes in jar lids and caught grasshoppers by day and fireflies at night. We pulled old bank forms out of the trash pit and played bank. In Granny Mae's front yard, there was a mimosa tree that was easy to climb, and it became my hotel. I would rent a room to Warren if he happened to be passing through. I always gave him an especially nice branch in exchange for his imaginary payment. In spring, my hotel was covered with pink flowers.

Warren and I played doctor. We were around ten years old, and the adults put us in the bathtub together. Unsupervised. For me and Warren, it was, "You show me yours and I'll show you mine." I had never seen a penis before, and he had probably never seen a vagina. Highly educational. And in such great contrast to my later experiences with Art. This was an innocent exploration, as opposed to a predatory attack.

The new owners of Granny Mae's place let me use their phone to call Warren. He was home, and he sounded happy to hear from me. We arranged to meet the next day.

Warren was wonderful. I was so happy to see him. He was over forty, but to me, he looked just the same as he had at eleven. His hair fell over his eyes no matter how many times he pushed it back. He was tall and big and moved around easily. He had a slow smile that was worth waiting for. Warren had recently gotten married. The three of us had lunch together and talked. During our conversation, Warren held the hand of his new wife. She was warm to me and lovely. Warren and I remembered things. He told me he was in recovery.

He got a worried look on his face, and his wife reached over and patted his hand, and told him to go ahead, it would be all right.

"I remember that I abused you sexually when we were younger in the bathtub." Warren made himself look at me as he talked, but I could see it was hard for him. He looked tortured, but I was glad that he had the courage to open up. I was touched by his concern and by how sincere he was.

But I told him that I didn't remember it the same way.

"Warren, in my memory we were just two kids exploring together. I never felt exploited or abused by you in any way." He relaxed as he heard my words. He had carried this guilty feeling for so many years, and he wasn't really guilty of anything.

"Thank you for saying that," he said. "I feel so much better hearing your words."

These were memories I was very sure of. "Warren, I never had any grudge against you for anything. I never felt you did anything that I wasn't interested in as well." I could tell he believed me and that a weight had lifted from him. I felt good for helping him come to this understanding.

Warren was in touch with the whole Athearn family. He called me the next day and gave me phone numbers and addresses for my mother's two sisters and her two brothers. I started by calling Aunt Doris's number since she was the oldest sister. My mother was in the middle, and Aunt Bet was the youngest.

Aunt Doris had moved to Tallulah Falls, Georgia, about a three-hour drive to the north. Tallulah Bankhead, the movie actress famous in the 1940s, had been named after the falls. I called Aunt Doris, and she sounded happy to hear from me. I drove up the next day.

Aunt Doris was now in her sixties. She seemed very wise and calm. Right away, she felt like a source of strength or me. We talked for hours. With Aunt Doris, I was able to verify my memories of the past. She told me that Art had indeed mistreated me from the day I had arrived.

I remembered that day. He and my mother had picked me up at the airport, and we got into his dark-green Buick. I remember the word "Dynaflow" in a scripty font along the side of the car, with three holes decorating each side of the Buick's hood.

There were a lot of gift-wrapped presents for me in the back seat. When Art gave me the gifts, I was sure that he was going to be nice to me. But within days, he criticized me for many things, like the way I had put my hand on my chair during meals. Things no one would ever even notice, Art found fault with.

Had I made it all up, his bad treatment of me, his constant criticism, even the molestation? My memories were so unusual and dramatic. But Doris confirmed that he resented me and treated me badly. I didn't mention the sex part. Aunt Doris was a devout Christian, and she was from an earlier generation. I sensed open talk about sex would make her very uncomfortable. But once again pieces of my memories were confirmed. Now, it did seem like the past I remembered had really happened.

I wanted to see my Aunt Bet as well, but she was living far away in southern Florida. Aunt Doris told me she was getting married in a few months, and she invited me to come back for her wedding and I could see my Aunt Bet there.

I will always be glad that I went to the wedding. It was a beautiful event. Aunt Doris married a sweet Baptist minister at a local Tallulah Falls church. The reception was in the church basement. It was very much in contrast with the over-the-top New York Jewish weddings I was used to. Punch bowls of ginger ale with scoops of pink sherbet in the middle were served. They served a new kind of tiny Ritz Cracker peanut butter sandwiches. These crackers immediately became a lifelong favorite food, always reminding me of Aunt Doris's wedding day.

At the wedding, when I saw my Aunt Bet for the first time since my mother's funeral, I felt close to her immediately. My mother's brothers and their children were at the wedding, also—uncles and more cousins.

In the coming years, I would visit many of them again and again. I had reconnected with the other half of my family. It felt like I had restored the missing half of my life story.

My Dad Dies

I was at the airport in record time, and the flight took forever. I jumped into a taxi and raced to the hospital. Back to the ICU. My 92-year-old dad looked pale and weak and smaller than he did the last time I saw him. I sat down and pulled the chair close to his bed. "Dad, I'm here," I told him. "And I'm staying." I saw his chest gently rising and falling, but his eyes didn't open, and he stayed still and silent.

The doctor said my dad had had a stroke in the night, and that he probably had no brain activity left. The doctor recommended that we not take any extreme measures to bring him back. He told me that it was time to let him go. Although my dad's wife was still alive, her dementia was advanced. Any decisions to be made would be mine.

I sat with my unconscious dad, holding his hand. He always liked having his hand held. I loved my dad a lot—he had been wonderful to me in so many ways. And even more than that, we had always had a special bond, a special connection, since I was young. Call me a daddy's girl, it was just a fact. I spent the whole day just sitting with him, talking to him at times, holding his hand. When it got late, I took a cab back to his house where I slept in the guest room. His wife was there, but she didn't remember that he was in the hospital.

She asked, "Where's Marvin?"

Moments of Knowing

"On a business trip," I told her. Explaining things would have just been cruel. She wouldn't remember it for more than two minutes, and it would just make her sad.

Day after day, I headed back to Hogue Hospital in Newport Beach, California. I sat with my unconscious dad each day. They had him on morphine, hooked up to all kinds of machines. There must have been twenty different lines going into his nose, his mouth, into the skin on the back of his hand, into his neck. I remembered a book by a physician who cited the "Five-line rule of the ICU." He stated that any patient with more than five lines was not going to make it. This scared me, and I put it out of my mind.

The next day, a nurse told me to squeeze his hand, and that he would squeeze back. I tried it, and he did. I was surprised. On some level he was alive in there and processing. I spoke to him. "It's OK, Dad. Just rest and relax. I'm here. I'm not leaving. I love you very much." From then on, I talked to him more.

Sometimes he grimaced and looked like he was in pain. I reported this to the nurse. She agreed with me that this was a sign of discomfort. The nurses were good at guessing what was wrong with him, and they worked to provide relief. The grimaces went away.

Hospital staff members continually came in and out of the room, all wearing color coded uniforms. Respiratory therapists wore light green scrubs and came in twice a day to check breathing and oxygen levels. Wound therapists wore maroon cotton and checked that a rash or a bed sore didn't get out of control. Social workers had on white jackets like doctors but no stethoscopes. They stopped in daily to check on my dad. Everything was mobilized to get him well, even though everyone knew he was not going to get well.

My Dad Dies

Nurses all wore navy blue. My dad's ICU nurse had only two patients, so she had time each day to talk with me about how he was doing. I saw his primary care MD once a day, as well as the "intensivist," a medical specialist just for intensive care patients. I became the advocate for my dad. I checked his state of health, moment by moment, as best I knew how. I asked questions: What drugs was he getting? Why? When would we know how his kidneys were doing? Why were they giving him that medicine? I tracked the crisis of the day.

When a family member gets sick, it's like going to medical school. There are so many new kinds of things to learn about: white counts, creatinine levels, kidney functions. What do those readouts on the computer monitor mean?

I learned that the undulating green sine wave was his heart pumping, and that the red numbers were his blood pressure.

All the clear plastic lines going into him were coming from a kind of tree of plastic bags that stood next to his bed. Each bag dripped its potion into him—antibiotics, sugar water, pain killers. Big red digital readouts on the tree told the nurses which bags were still good and which needed replacement.

After a few days, Dad got pneumonia and had become septic. I knew the word "septic," but I didn't understand what it meant as a condition. I went "back to medical school" and learned sepsis happened when bacteria from an illness got into the blood. At that point, the blood pumped the bacteria through all the organs. If sepsis wasn't reversed, one by one all the organs failed.

Every day, another one of my dad's systems failed. Anxiously I awaited word about how serious each failure was, what to expect, and what his chances were. Not good. I began to accept that this was really the end.

Moments of Knowing

From time to time, he would suddenly regain consciousness for a few moments. One day he opened his eyes, looked right at me, and said, "I'm dying."

"Close, Dad, but no cigar," I said, hoping I was correct, wanting to encourage him. "Close but no cigar" was one of our favorite shared quips. He smiled at me, happy to awaken, however briefly, to a world where people were still cracking jokes. But then he shut his eyes and went back to his otherworldly state.

Another day he woke up when the nurse came into the room. She saw he was awake and asked him, "Are you Marvin Fein?"

My dad answered without a moment's hesitation, "At your cervix, ma'am." She didn't hear it, but I did. How could she have missed it with that twinkle in his eye? But the twinkle didn't last long, and he soon closed his eyes again.

These conscious moments frightened me. How could he have no brain activity when he could crack a joke with perfect timing? I asked the doctor next time he came in.

"It's not unusual for patients like your dad to have lucid moments. But don't let that fool you. He's not going to return to his old self. We could take extreme measures to bring him back, but he is not going to be able to sit up, he's not going to be able to eat, talk, or have a real life. It's time to let go."

I didn't like it, but the doctor was clear. My dad had a DNR order: Do Not Resuscitate. The DNR stated his wishes, basically "Don't keep me alive by extreme measures." Still, I was the one who would make the call. What I really wanted to say to the doctors was, "Yes, of course you should save him, dammit! Do everything in your power to keep him alive! This is my dad! This is a wonderful man, warm, kind, full of energy and humor and good will! I don't care what it takes! Keep him going!"

I didn't say any of that, but a small part of me will forever wish I had. I didn't say anything because I knew it wasn't the time to hang on. It was the time to let him go. I fought the doubting voices as best I could. I tried reason. *It would be wrong to keep him alive. He would never be himself again, according to the best medical opinion. There is a time to die. For everything a season. Time to let go. You are doing the right thing. Don't torture yourself with what-ifs.* I had this same conversation with myself over and over.

Soon, they moved my dad to a special floor of the hospital that functioned as a hospice. There were no more efforts to save him. This was where they brought patients to die. I continued to sit with him day by day. He had one tube left, just morphine that kept him comfortable. No food, no fluids, no medicines. No more parade of workers in colorful uniforms trying to save him. Just me and him, and a nurse who checked once in a while to make sure he was comfortable. The monitor still showed the sine wave, curving up and curving down, the ongoing trace of life.

I held his hand. I thought back over his life. He had always told his stories over and over, and I knew them all by heart. I can still hear them.

"You were such a cute little girl with that button nose. You learned how to sing 'Ramblin' Wreck from Georgia Tech' when you were four years old. You were so adorable singing that song."

He would go on. "How much I loved the South! Do you remember that we went to see *Gone with the Wind* four times?"

"Yes, Dad, four times before I was even twelve years old. I'll never forget. Tara is in my blood, forever."

During his last years, he didn't realize that he was telling the same stories over and over. Almost every day he would ask me, "Did I ever tell you how I met your mother?"

Only three times a week for quite a few years now . . .

"No, Dad, please tell me how you met my mother." All this would be in front of wife number three. *Oh well. Her dementia is so bad, I don't think she understands. And if she does, I hope she will forget it all in five minutes.*

Dad would launch into the story about meeting my mother, always starting with "It was love at first sight." He would tell me how his lab partner Mitchell had recently become engaged and wanted to go on a double date. The lab partner offered to bring his sister to be my dad's date. The sister was young, only sixteen.

"She wore a dark red, plaid woolen dress. The minute she stepped out of the car, I fell in love with her. She was the most beautiful girl I had ever seen. It was love at first sight."

I love it that my parents had a beautiful beginning, regardless of the rest.

One day at the hospital, I got a feeling he was hanging on, refusing to let go. I spoke out loud. "Dad don't be afraid. You can go anytime you want. It'll be okay. I'll be okay." I continued, "As close as you and I are now, that's how it will be forever. Nothing can ever change that. I'll help take care of your wife. I know you worry about her. She'll be okay. Don't hang around here just because you're worried about us. We'll be fine."

I pulled my chair closer to the bed and reached out my hand to squeeze his hand one more time. I kept talking to him. "You have nothing to worry about. You have lived a wonderful life, full of goodness and honesty and kindness. Remember all the good things. Remember how you enjoyed talking with all those people you had never met before in restaurants and on elevators and on the streets of New York. How you loved talking to strangers all your life. How you made so many friends, and so many good friends. Remember how you loved a great corned beef sandwich with a cup of matzo ball soup. Remember the good things. You will always be safe because you are a good man."

I kept holding his hand. I mentally recorded my picture

of him for playback, for my memories. I felt his life force, still emanating. I felt our bond and our connection, the energies between us so strong. And so fortunate.

I remembered another of his stories, about how he got lost when he was only ten. His mother had taken all the kids to Macy's Herald Square on 34th Street, and somehow, my dad had gotten separated in the crowd.

"I had a dime and a subway token," he always explained. "I used the dime to call home from a pay phone. But the new housekeeper didn't speak English, and all she could say was, 'Missy no home, missy no home.'"

How many times have I heard how he found the subway, how he put his token into the slot and rode all the way home, more than an hour's ride, all the way to the end of the line at 242nd and Broadway. How he walked up the hill to the house. Such a resourceful kid. He knew what to do when he was lost.

I continued to give him permission to go. To let go of us, to move on. "You'll know what to do. It will be like Macy's Herald Square. You won't be lost. You'll find the way. And I will be with you forever. You and I each have a cosmic dime that will let us call one another anytime just by thinking about it. And a cosmic subway token that will always bring us to the same place together. Nothing can separate us. Not death. Not life. You will be my new angel, watching over me, keeping me safe. Take off, Dad. Let go. Fly."

I left the hospital in the late afternoon. I got to his house and his wife came to me and said, "Guess who visited me when I took a nap? Marvin! Marvin came and paid a visit to me, wasn't that nice of him? I was so happy to see him. I'm sure he'll come home for good soon."

It scared me that he had come to her in a dream. I picked up the phone and called the hospital nursing station.

Moments of Knowing

"How's my dad doing?" I asked the nurse when she picked up.

A pause. And then she said, "He passed away just one minute ago. I was with him. I can't believe your timing. You must have known somehow. Do you want to come back and visit with him one last time?"

I thought for a minute and then said no. I thanked her and hung up the phone. Now he was really gone. I couldn't see him again. I felt no need to go and look at his body. Everything was set up with the funeral home, so there was nothing to do.

A new world, with no father. A person who had always been here in this world with me, every minute of my life until now. Someone who held up the sky. It would have been easy if I resented him, hated him, didn't like him. But I loved him, knew him as a good man, a gentleman's gentleman. An honest businessman. Enthusiastic about life, always. Funny. Kind. Interested. Always wanting the very best for me.

I didn't know what to do next. I decided to get on the phone and let everyone who loved him know. Anything else could wait.

The family in New York. I called every one of them, and each of them was wonderful. My dad's last remaining sister was sharp and wise and somehow managed to hold me close, even over the phone and across the continent. She comforted me. My wonderful cousins told me how right I was to let him go, not to try extreme measures to save him.

Locally, there were his wife's kids. They would miss him, too. The step siblings and I agreed to have a memorial a few months later on Dad's birthday, in August. He loved California, and he wanted his ashes tossed into the Pacific Ocean. We planned to take a little boat out and each pour some of him into the sea. This felt right. I flew home after a few days.

My Dad Dies

Once home, I entered the world of the grieving. I would go along, and then suddenly something would remind me, and the tears would come. Gentle ambushes. Unexpected emotional arrivals set off by a phrase, by a thought, by the simplest things. I wore his watch, and then it stopped. This threw me into a panic. I took it to a watch repair store and asked them to put in a new battery.

The man behind the counter looked at the watch and said, "Lady, you have to wind it."

Oh yeah, I remember watches that need winding! Thank heaven it wasn't not broken. It just stopped. There was no battery. I wound it up and was happy to see the hands moving once again. It was almost a reincarnation.

In the drug store they were selling Father's Day cards. I wouldn't be buying those anymore. In a way, I didn't mind the grieving. It was sweet and sad and had hollow feeling, but it was OK. There was kindness there. I gave thanks for my father's wisdom and for the lifetime of love he gave me.

He protects me from beyond the grave with his gentle spirit. I know you are there, Dad. I love you so much.

My Religion
Is Kindness

I think the most important thing in the world is being kind. Being kind to other people and to all creatures. Being kind to oneself. I first realized the importance of kindness when I was the five-year-old being bullied on the playground, and the realization has grown throughout my life.

This has always felt like one of life's most important teachings. It sounds so simple. You have probably heard the Dalai Lama say, "My religion is kindness." Maybe it sounds like a bumper sticker, but I don't care about that. It's still my fundamental truth.

For a long time, I thought the most important thing in life was to be present. To wake up to the moment and be aware of my entire situation, my inner state, my outer actions, the other people in the picture, the air on my skin. Just being present.

I worked to be present as much as possible but was successful only a small percentage of the time. However, this was still my primary goal and primary value. Then, gradually I felt something was missing with just being present, with working to be equanimous as much as possible with anything and everything that was happening in the moment. Sometimes that equanimity would go over the line into indifference. It didn't feel complete.

Then, it changed. For me, life is still about being present, but now I want to be present with warmth, welcoming everything that shows up in the moment. Can I be present to everything that's going on, no matter how big or how small? Can I be present with curiosity, interest, and enthusiasm? I live such a lucky life, a life mostly without want or hunger or violence. Most of the time what's going on around me is wholesome and healthy.

It started with me wanting to bring warmth to the people in my life, to the people with whom I found myself: friends, family, those in line with me at the grocery store. But then it expanded, and I began to feel warmth for everything in my life, even objects and difficult situations.

Like the little clock I am trying to fix and getting so frustrated with that I want to throw it and its parts at the wall? Can I back up and find warmth for that little clock? It's living here in the same universe as me. Can I embrace everything in my world as if it were part of a configuration that is holding me and making my life?

Warmth for things. We don't really know what things are. We assume humans are the only conscious beings, the only beings capable of kindness. I have often thought that kindness is the distinguishing, beautiful mark of our humanity.

But lately I wonder if rocks and other small things, galaxies and other big things, and all "things" and "objects," both large and small, are actually conscious beings like us. We don't know. They could be. Maybe rocks reside in a slower time frame that we can't communicate with. This makes sense to me. Can I bring warmth to the rocks?

Sometimes—well, probably a lot of the time—I can see I am not totally wholesome, not totally healthy. We are all so imperfect, and many a moment finds me feeling negative about something. Perhaps I am hurrying to get to the next moment as if this moment had no value. Perhaps I am working with a negative emotion, something that is demanding to be let out. Greed, wanting more, wanting it now. Or, anger, reaction, contention.

How do I get back to the warmth when a present moment has these rough elements? Sometimes it's just too hard. But I believe that if I can work on it, I can find the way back. Every time I find the way back to warmth and kindness, I'm walking my chosen path through this world, learning where to turn right and when to double back and when that warmth is just around the corner. Next time, I will know the way a little better. Warmth GPS.

Sometimes, I am not sure about how to be present. People can be annoying or even violent. How to be present to that? And it's not just other people, it's me, too. Whenever I feel ill will toward someone else, whenever someone makes me angry and I want to push back at them, there's violence in that. Isn't it true that when we want to push back, we basically want the other person to suffer and get a dose of their own medicine? Wanting someone to suffer is the definition of cruelty. If I can remember ill will has cruelty at its center, maybe I can be more careful. Maybe I can transform it into something else.

For me, there is a clear key to being present to someone who is unaware or angry or unpleasant. That key is to bring compassion. Compassion for the one I am feeling ill will toward because it is likely the person who is annoying me so much is suffering. Why else would they behave so mindlessly, so destructively? They don't realize it, but they are suffering. Can I realize it even if they don't? Can I bring compassion? And when I feel ill will, can I bring compassion to myself and know that feeling ill will is sometimes just part of being human? Being a human being?

Compassion is so close to kindness. It's kindness toward the other person when the other person is suffering. Their pain changes the energy of the loving-kindness. It's no longer just loving and light, no longer just pure friendliness. Now there is sadness. Deep and heartfelt.

Compassion empathizes, wants to be one with the person who is suffering, wants to understand their state of mind, feel what they are feeling. How can I do all that, be with what they are feeling, without taking on their suffering? The key is to bring in equanimity. Equanimity will keep us from taking on the other person's suffering in the same destructive and painful way that they have taken it on. Once we do that, we are incapable of compassion. We become as lost as they are. With equanimity, we can be at one with the person, at one with their suffering, bringing understanding to them and goodwill.

It takes believing that every person is good by nature and the person suffering is essentially the same as me. But they've been hurt. They have fallen on hard times. That's why they are violent. That's why they are acting badly.

I saw the movie *Dune* recently. I remembered a line from the novel, which I read and loved in the 1960s. The line is, "Fear is the mind killer." I always felt this was such a helpful idea.

For example, on airplanes, I sometimes get afraid in turbulence. I am frightened when the plane's uncontrolled movements move my body about uncontrollably, even if the movements are small. I have learned that when this fear arises, I need to close my eyes and pay attention to my breathing. I've done this so many times on so many airplanes, and every time, the fear is gone in only a few minutes. The fear gets replaced by an absolute willingness to die right now. If this is my time, if this is it, I am ready. Bring it on. I am remembering, "Fear is the mind killer."

Buddhism is said to have two wings, the wing of wisdom and the wing of compassion. Being present to things as they are is the wing of wisdom . . . seeing what are called the three marks of existence: everything is constantly changing; there is great suffering in the world; and my sense of self is inflated and exaggerated and there may be no self at all. The wing of wisdom is being present . . . being present to these marks of our existence.

The wing of compassion is being present with a soft and warm heart to all beings everywhere, known and unknown, seen and unseen, born and to be born.

May all beings be safe and peaceful, healthy and happy. And may I be kind.

Acknowledgments

Many thanks to my Gold Country Writing group sisters, Patti Bess, Emma Wall, Shelley Wagner, and past group members Mary Gorden and others. I would never have written my books without the help of these fellow writers. My life and all my efforts are especially blessed by a close circle of long-time friends: Constance, Kathy, Patty, Christy, Jody, Debbie, Harry, Rory, David, Scott, Mark, and Ron.

For some reason these friends believe I can write books! Much appreciation for the great loving-kindness of my Buddhist friends at Mountain Stream Meditation: John, Marcia, Robyn, Jen, Juanita, Tony, Rev. Helen, and the whole meditating gang. I have so many kind and generous people in my life, and I feel boundless gratitude to them. They make my writing possible.

Author Bio

Mary Helen Fein was born in Riverdale, New York, in 1943. She attended schools in New York, and she has a B.A. in English Literature from Temple University, an MS in Computer Science Engineering from the University of Pennsylvania, and for two years, she studied painting at the Pennsylvania Academy of Fine Arts, America's oldest art school. Mary Helen is a Certified Zentangle Teacher and holds small classes in this meditative art form. In addition, she has trained extensively and is authorized to teach Insight Meditation. She is active in her local Buddhist community, Mountain Stream Meditation, and served on their non-profit Board of Directors. Mary Helen is a Buddhist Community Dharma Leader and often gives talks and leads sitting groups and meditation classes. She lives in Northern California where she writes, paints, and draws.

Looking for your next great read?

We can help!

Visit www.shewritespress.com/next-read
or scan the QR code below for a list
of our recommended titles.

She Writes Press is an award-winning
independent publishing company founded to
serve women writers everywhere.